THE GIRL WHO MARRIED A LION

Alexander McCall Smith

WINDSOR
PARAGON

First published 2004 by
Canongate Books Ltd
This Large Print edition published 2005 by
BBC Audiobooks Ltd by arrangement with
Canongate Books Ltd

ISBN 1 4056 1113 8 (Windsor Hardcover)
ISBN 1 4056 2100 1 (Paragon Softcover)

The following stories first published in
The Girl Who Married a Lion in 2004
A Bad Way to Treat Friends, Bad Uncles,
Lazy Baboons,
The Grandmother Who Was Kind to a Smelly Girl,
The Thathana Moratho Tree, Tremendously Clever
Tricks are Played, But to Limited Effect
Copyright © Alexander McCall Smith 2004

Other stories first published in *Children of Wax* in 1989
by Canongate Books Ltd
Copyright © Alexander McCall Smith 1989

British Library Cataloguing in Publication Data available

Printed and bound in Great Britain by
Antony Rowe Ltd., Chippenham, Wiltshire

For Finola O'Sullivan

CONTENTS

Introduction

This is a collection of traditional stories from two countries in Africa—Zimbabwe and Botswana. Although these differ in ethnic and linguistic terms, they share many of the folk tales which are found throughout neighbouring countries of Southern Africa. This sharing of oral literature is not uncommon. Folk tales throughout the world have a striking number of common features, and many familiar themes crop up in folk traditions that are culturally very different. In a sense, then, these tales are part of a universal language which can speak to people across human frontiers, just as music does.

There are many fine collections of sub-Saharan African folk tales, many of them compiled by scholars of oral literature. I do not count myself amongst such experts—far from it—and this collection therefore makes very modest claims. In order to present the stories in a way which will interest and entertain a broad readership, I have deliberately taken certain liberties with re-telling, added some descriptions of landscape, and deepened the treatment of certain emotions. I hope that in doing so I have been able to bring out the beauty and poetry of these stories. A word-for-word transcription would not necessarily do them justice in that respect.

I collected many of these stories myself some twenty years ago in the southern part of Zimbabwe known as Matabeleland. These stories were told to me—with the assistance of an interpreter—by people living in the Matopos hills, to the south of Bulawayo. They were also recounted to me by people in Bulawayo itself. Sometimes they were told by old people—by grandmothers—sometimes by children. It was a particular pleasure to hear the stories from children, as they told them with such spirit and enjoyment. All of these stories were recounted to me with generosity and warmth—qualities which those who know that part of Africa, or even just visit it briefly, will recognise as being so typical of the people there. I have expanded this original collection of stories, published some years ago under the title *Children of Wax*, to include stories from Botswana. These stories were obtained for me from people living in the Mochudi and Odi areas of Botswana. They were collected by Elinah Grant, a friend of mine, who runs a small museum in Mochudi. Elinah translated the stories from Setswana into English, and I am most grateful to her for her labours. Again,

I have retold them, using some of the original language and some of mine.

And what wonderful things are contained in these stories! Not only do we find all the familiar human emotions—jealousy, ambition, love—but we see moral rules set out very clearly. We see loyalty rewarded; we see greed punished; we see the encouragement of those values of community which are so important in Africa and from which we can learn so much. But we are shown more than that: we are introduced to a fascinating world view in which the boundaries between the animal and human worlds are indistinct and fluid. This is a traditional African vision, but it is also something very modern that we are only beginning to understand in Western countries. We are not the masters of nature—we are part of it.

The two countries from which these stories are drawn are remarkable places. The people who inhabit them are generous-spirited and have a superb sense of humour. In these stories we are afforded a glimpse of the values and traditions that have made their societies so extraordinary. They speak to us from the African heart. I count myself fortunate indeed that I have been given the chance to hear them and to help pass them on to others. But the stories remain the property and creation of those who told them to me, and any credit for these is theirs alone.

But let us pass from these serious matters to the true business of this book. How can a girl possibly have married a lion? How can a man have a tree growing out of his head? And how can a woman have children made of wax? The stories in this collection make these questions seem simple, everyday ones—with, as it happens, simple, everyday answers.

Alexander McCall Smith
Edinburgh 2004

A Letter From Mma Ramotswe

When I was a very young girl in Mochudi I listened to stories just like the ones in this book. They were told to me by my father's aunt, who was very old then, and who is now late. She was a very kind woman, and she knew many stories, which she had told to my father, Obed Ramotswe, when he was a small boy. That is how these stories are remembered in Botswana, and in many other countries in Africa.

When I hear these stories they make me sad. That is not because they are stories of sad things that have happened, it is because they remind me of the Africa of my childhood and of all the good things that there were then. Everybody feels a little bit sad when they think of their childhood, because the world we knew then seems so far away. Looking back is like looking through a window which is covered with dust: you can just make out the faces, but nothing is very clear.

But then you hear these old stories—the stories that you heard so many times—and suddenly everything comes back. You are there again, sitting with your aunt outside her house, and it is quiet, and the sky is empty and the sun is on the land. And you think: I am a lucky person to be here, to be listening to these things that happened in another place, just round the corner, in the days when the animals could speak. And the sadness goes away and your heart is full again.

I shall put this book on my desk and read it when there is nothing much to be done in the No.1 Ladies' Detective Agency. And I shall choose one of the stories and ask my assistant, Mma Makutsi, whether she remembers it. And she will laugh, and say yes, and we shall think about that story while the kettle is boiling and we are preparing our tea. That is what we shall do.

Precious Ramotswe,
No. 1 Ladies' Detective Agency,
behind Tlokweng Road Speedy Motors,
Tlokweng Road,
Gaborone, Botswana

THE GIRL WHO MARRIED A LION

Guinea Fowl Child

A rich man like Mzizi, who had many cattle, would normally be expected to have many children. Unhappily, his wife, Pitipiti, was unable to produce children. She consulted many people about this, but although she spent much on charms and medicines that would bring children, she remained barren.

Pitipiti loved her husband and it made her sad to see his affection for her vanishing as he waited for the birth of children. Eventually, when it was clear that she was not a woman for bearing a child, Pitipiti's husband married another wife. Now he lived in the big kraal with his new young wife and Pitipiti heard much laughter coming from the new wife's hut. Soon there was a first child, and then another.

Pitipiti went to take gifts to the children, but she was rebuffed by the new wife.

'For so many years Mzizi wasted his time with you,' the new wife mocked. 'Now in just a short time I have given him children. We do not want your gifts.'

She looked for signs in her husband's eyes of the love that he used to show for her, but all she saw was the pride that he felt on being the

1

father of children. It was as if she no longer existed for him. Her heart cold within her, Pitipiti made her way back to her lonely hut and wept. What was there left for her to live for now—her husband would not have her and her brothers were far away. She would have to continue living by herself and she wondered whether she would be able to bear such loneliness.

Some months later, Pitipiti was ploughing her fields when she heard a cackling noise coming from some bushes nearby. Halting the oxen, she crept over to the bushes and peered into them. There, hiding in the shade, was a guinea fowl. The guinea fowl saw her and cackled again.

'I am very lonely,' he said. 'Will you make me your child?'

Pitipiti laughed. 'But I cannot have a guinea fowl for my child!' she exclaimed. 'Everyone would laugh at me.'

The guinea fowl seemed rather taken aback by this reply, but he did not give up.

'Will you make me your child just at night?' he asked. 'In the mornings I can leave your hut very early and nobody will know.'

Pitipiti thought about this. Certainly this would be possible: if the guinea fowl was out of the hut by the time the sun arose, then nobody need know that she had adopted it. And it would be good, she thought, to have a child, even if it was really a guinea fowl.

'Very well,' she said, after a few moments' reflection. 'You can be my child.'

The guinea fowl was delighted and that evening, shortly after the sun had gone down, he came to Pitipiti's hut. She welcomed him and made him an evening meal, just as any mother would do with her child. They were both very happy.

Still the new wife laughed at Pitipiti. Sometimes she would pass by Pitipiti's fields and jeer at her, asking her why she grew crops if she had no mouths to feed. Pitipiti ignored these jibes, but inside her every one of them was like a small sharp spear that cuts and cuts.

The guinea fowl heard these taunts from a tree in which he was sitting, and he cackled with rage. For the new wife, though, these sounds were just the sound of a bird in a tree.

'Mother,' the guinea fowl asked that night. 'Why do you bear the insults of that other woman?'

Pitipiti could think of no reply to this. In truth there was little that she could do. If she tried to chase away the new wife, then her husband would be angry with her and might send her away altogether. There was nothing she could do.

The bird, however, thought differently. He was not going to have his mother insulted in this way and the following day he arose early and flew to the highest tree that overlooked the fields of the new wife. There, as the sun arose, he called out a guinea fowl song:

> Come friends, there is grain to eat!
> Come and eat all this woman's grain!

It did not take long for the new wife to realize what was happening. Shouting with anger, she ran out into the fields and killed Pitipiti's guinea fowl and his friends. Then she took them back to her hut, plucked out their feathers, and began to cook them.

Mzizi was called to the feast and together he and his new wife ate all the guinea fowl at one sitting. It was a tasty meal and they were both very pleased with themselves for having made such a good start to the day.

No sooner had they finished the last morsel than Mzizi and the new wife heard the sound of singing coming from their stomachs. It was the guinea fowls singing their guinea fowl songs. This, of course, frightened the couple and they immediately seized long knives and stabbed at their stomachs to stop the noise. As the knives pierced their skins, bright blood flowed freely and they fell to the ground. As they fell, from out of the wounds came the guinea fowl and his friends, cackling with joy at their freedom. Soon they were back in the field, eating the last of the grain that was left.

Pitipiti was pleased that she no longer had to suffer the taunts of the new wife. She now owned her husband's cattle and because of this there were many men waiting to marry her. All of them, of course, were happy at the thought that they might marry a wife who had such a clever and unusual child.

A Bad Way To Treat Friends

It used to be that Leopard, Goat, Guinea Fowl and Wild Cat were all good friends. They lived together in the same place, near some hills that came out of the plains, and where there was good water and cool places to sleep.

Goat had some very fine children, of which she was justly proud. There were strong and healthy and they could stand on their back legs and eat the leaves from the shrubs that other animals could not reach. They were very clever children, too, and knew a lot about the world, which made other children envious. Leopard's children were not very strong. They could not run as fast as leopard children normally run, and their coats were dull and matted.

When Leopard saw Goat's children playing in the grass, her heart was filled with hatred for them. These children made her own children look so thin and weak that she wished that they could be got rid of. In that way her own children would be the healthiest and strongest children in that place. But how was she to get Goat to go away for long enough for her to deal with Goat's children? The idea came to her that she would ask Goat to go and

7

look for a new dress for her, as she had been invited—or so she would say—to a party to be held by her cousins.

Goat agreed to Leopard's request, and she went off to the other side of the river to look for a fine new dress for her friend, Leopard. She left her children behind, telling them not to wander away but to stay within sight of Leopard, who would look after them. These strong children, who were also very obedient, agreed to do what their mother had asked them. All the time, Leopard was watching this, watching, watching.

Once Goat had gone, Leopard crouched down and began to stalk Goat's children through the long grass. The poor children, not knowing the danger that was now so close to them, were full of happiness. Then, in an instant, Leopard was upon them. She seized them and carried them back to her place by the scruff of their necks. The children thought that this must be a game, as Leopard was their mother's friend, and they continued to laugh and smile even as they were dragged along.

Once she had captured all the children, Leopard tied up their mouths and wrapped them in leaves. Now they were bundles ready to take off to the party, where Leopard and her cousins would eat them. Unknown to Leopard, though, Guinea Fowl and Wild Cat had returned from a journey, and they watched in dismay as they saw what Leopard was doing. They were saddened by the thought that Goat's happy children would no longer be jumping up and down in the grass and singing their goat songs that they all so liked to hear. They could not believe that Leopard would be wicked enough to do such a thing, but now they saw it all before their very eyes.

Shortly afterwards, Goat returned from the other side of the river, bearing a fine new dress which she had bought for Leopard. Leopard was very pleased with this, as she was a vain person who liked to wear fine dresses and admire her reflection in the water.

While Leopard was busy trying on her new dress, Guinea Fowl and Wild Cat crept round to the place where the parcels were stored and they took the leaves off Goat's children.

'You must go and hide,' they said to the children. 'Make sure that Leopard doesn't see you, though, for she is very wicked.'

Goat's children, shocked by what had happened to them, went off into the bushes, stifling their tears as they did so. Guinea Fowl and Wild Cat did not go with them, as they had business to do. Seeing Leopard's children nearby, they went over to them and very quickly overpowered them. It was not difficult to do that, as Leopard's children were weak and sickly. Then they wrapped them in leaves—the very leaves which only a short time

9

ago had been wrapped around Goat's children.

It was now time for everybody to set off to the party. Leopard, who was pleased with herself in her new dress, did not bother to find out where her children were and had no idea that they were inside the parcels which she was carrying. So when Guinea Fowl and Wild Cat asked her what was in these parcels, she replied only that there was good meat for them to have at the party.

When they arrived at the party, Leopard told her cousins that they should put the parcels into the pot unopened. She did not want Goat, who was there, to see that her children were being put into the pot. Guinea Fowl, though, realised the danger that they were in, and she whispered to Goat and Wild Cat that they should all run away before the parcels were taken out of the pot.

Later when Leopard took out the parcels and opened them, she saw that her own children were inside and had been cooked. This made her cry out in anger and run back to their place by the hills, so that she might catch Goat and her children and punish them. But they had left by the time she got there, and that is why even to this day we see leopards searching for goats.

A Girl Who Lived In A Cave

A girl who only had one brother liked the place where she and her parents lived. There was a river nearby, where she could draw water, and the family's cattle enjoyed the sweet grass which grew by the riverside. The huts were shaded from the hot sun by the broad leaves of the trees, and at night there was a soft breeze from the hills, which kept them cool. Passers-by, who called in to drink water from the family's calabashes, would say how much they envied that quiet place, and how their own places were so much drier and dustier.

Then a terrible thing happened, which spoiled the happiness of the family. The girl had gone to fetch water from the river and was walking back to her hut with a large calabash on her head. Suddenly she began to feel that she was being followed. At first she did nothing, but then, when the feeling became quite strong, she turned round and looked behind her. There was nothing to be seen, although the tall grass moved and there was a faint sound, rather like that which a creature makes when it scurries through a bush.

The girl continued on her way. After she had taken a few more steps she again heard a noise. This time she swung round more sharply, dropping the calabash to the ground. There was a man behind her, crouching down, half in the grass, half out of it.

The girl was frightened by the sight of the man, but she tried not to show her fear. He smiled at her, and rose to his feet.

'You must not be afraid of me,' he said. 'I am just walking in the grass.'

The girl could not understand why a man should wish to walk in the grass, but she did not say anything. The man came up to her and reached out to touch her.

'You are a nice, fat girl,' he said.

The girl was now very nervous and moved away from the man's touch.

'My father's place is just there,' she said. 'I can see the smoke from his fire.'

The man looked in the direction of the huts.

'If that is so,' he said, 'I can walk with you to your father's place, where I can eat some food.'

The girl walked ahead of the man and soon they came to the circle of huts under the trees. There the stranger waited at the gate while the girl went in to tell her father that there was a man who wished to eat some food. The father came out, called to the man, and invited him to sit on a stone under one of the trees. Food

12

was made by the girl's mother and given to the man. He took it, and put it all into his mouth in one piece. Then he swallowed, and all the food was gone. The girl had not seen a man eat in this way before and wondered why he should be so hungry.

After the man had eaten, he got up and said goodbye to the father. He looked around him before he left, as if he was trying to remember what the family looked like and what they owned. Then he walked off and was soon obscured by the tall grass that grew in that part.

The girl went to stand by her father's side.

'That was a very wicked man,' said the father. 'I am very sorry that he visited this place.'

'I am sure he will not come back,' the girl said. 'He was going somewhere else when I met him.'

The father shook his head sadly.

'Now that he is here,' he said. 'We shall have to leave. I shall tell your brother to collect his sleeping mat and get ready for us to go to some other place.'

*   *   *

The girl could not believe that the family would be leaving the place where they had lived for so long and of which she felt so fond.

She tried to persuade her father to stay, but he was convinced that they were in great danger by staying where they were.

'It is better to move now,' he said, 'than to regret it later.'

The girl wept, but her tears were ignored by her father. Soon he had all the family's possessions loaded on his back and was calling out to the others to follow him on the path.

'I shall not come with you,' the girl said defiantly. 'I have been happy in this place and see no reason to move.'

The girl's mother pleaded with her to go, but the girl refused. Eventually the father became impatient.

'If you must stay,' he said, 'then you should at least go and live in a cave in the hillside. There is a place there where there is a large rock which can be used as a door. At night you must roll that rock in behind you and let nobody into the cave.'

The girl agreed to this, as she knew that nearby cave. It was comfortable and cool, and she thought she would be happy there. As the rest of the family disappeared down the path that led to their new place, she took her mat and her pots to the cave and set them on a ledge at the back. Then, since it was beginning to get dark, she rolled the rock in the front into position. Inside the cave, it was pitch black, but the girl felt safe and she slept well that first night.

*   *   *

The next day, the girl's brother paid her a visit
to see how she was. She told him of how
comfortable she had been in the cave and of
how well she had slept.

'I am safe there,' she explained. 'The rock
blocks the mouth of the cave and I shall open
it to nobody. If you come, though, you should
sing this song and I shall know that it is you.'

The girl then sang a short song, which the
boy listened to. He kept the words in his mind,
as he planned to visit the girl that night to
make sure that she was safe and that the rock
was acting as a strong enough door.

That evening, when he returned, it was
already dark. As he approached the cave, he
sang the song which she had taught him:

> There is a rock here and the cave is dark;
> Open the cave, my sister, and let me in.

When the girl heard this song, she knew
straight away that her brother was outside. She
pushed at the rock and it rolled to one side.
Her brother was pleased to see that the song
worked and that his sister was safe. He gave
her the food that he had brought her and then
said goodbye.

15

'Make sure that you roll the rock back once I am outside,' he said.

'I shall always remember that,' his sister replied. 'A girl could not live alone in a cave like this unless she had a rock for protection.'

*   *   *

The brother came the next day, and the day after that. On his third visit there was something that worried him. Not far from the cave he noticed that there were footprints on the ground and that lying nearby there was a bone which had been gnawed. He picked up the bone and looked at it. Whoever had eaten it must have had a great appetite, for his teeth had cut right into the bone to extract its goodness. The footprints were large, too, and the sight of them made the brother feel uneasy.

He arrived at the front of the cave and began to sing his song. As he did so, he had a strange feeling—as if there was somebody watching him. He turned round, but all that he saw was the wind moving through the dry brown grass and a rain bird circling in the sky. He finished the song, and the girl rolled back the rock to let him into the cave.

'I would like you to come and live with your family again,' he said to the girl. 'We are sad that you are not with us.'

16

'I am sorry too,' she replied. 'And yet I love this place too much to leave it. Perhaps one day my father will decide to come back here.'

The boy shook his head. He knew that his father would never come back now that he had found that he liked the other place to which he had gone. Soon the memory of this place would fade and the family would talk no more about it.

The boy ate some food with his sister and then left. As he walked away, he again felt that there was somebody watching him, but again he saw nothing but the wind and a small snake that moved like a dark arrow through the dry leaves on the ground.

*   *   *

The man who had driven the family away from that place was a cannibal. Now he had heard the boy singing his special song to his sister in the cave and he had remembered the words. Under a large tree not far away, he practiced the song which the boy sang. His voice, though, was too rough, and he realized that no girl would be fooled into believing that it was the voice of her young brother.

The cannibal had a way to deal with this. He made a fire, and on the fire he put a number of stones. Then, when these stones were red hot, he put them in his mouth and let them lie

17

against that part of his throat that made the sound. After a few minutes he spat out the stones and tried the song again. The stones had done what he had hoped they would do and his voice was now as soft as the boy's.

Inside the cave, the girl had settled herself to sleep on her sleeping mat when she heard her brother singing outside. It surprised her that he should come back so soon, but then she remembered that he had left a calabash in the cave and might be returning to collect it.

'I am coming, my brother,' the girl sang out. 'The rock will move back and let you in.'

*   *   *

By the time that the mouth of the cave was half open, the girl realized that it was not her brother who was standing outside. When she saw the cannibal, her heart gave a leap of fear and she struggled to roll the rock back. The cannibal, though, was too quick and had seized her before she could seal off the cave mouth.

The girl screamed as the cannibal lifted her off the ground and began to tie her arms and legs with a rope he had with him. Then, when she was firmly tied up, he went to a place nearby and began to make a fire so that he could cook the girl and eat her. As he made the fire, he sang a special song, of the sort that cannibals sing, in which he told of how a poor hungry cannibal had found a fat girl in a cave.

The girl wept with sorrow at the thought of what had happened to her. She wept for her father and mother, whom she would never see again, and she wept for her stupidity in trying to stay in so dangerous a place. Through her tears, she sang a sad song, about how a girl who lived in a cave was captured by a wicked cannibal.

*   *   *

The boy had felt so uneasy on his way home that he had come back to the cave. Now he was hiding in the grass, listening to the sad song of his sister. When he saw the cannibal bending over his fire, the boy rushed forward and pushed him into the flames. The many skins which the cannibal was wearing soon caught fire and he ran wildly away, letting out strange cries as he ran.

The boy untied his sister and then led her back to their father's new place. That night, the girl told her father of what had happened. He was worried at the thought of the narrow escape that she had had, but he was relieved that she was now safe. He was glad, too, to hear that the cannibal had run away, as this meant that the family could now return to that place where they had been so happy, and where the girl knew they would be happy once again.

Hare Fools The Baboons

A clever hare realized that the lion was always welcomed by the other animals. This was not because the other animals liked the lion; it was because they were all afraid of him. If the lion came to another animal's house then it was wisest to give him a lot of food. If the hare ever went to another animal's house, then he was more likely to be told to go away.

'This is unfair,' the hare said to himself. 'I could do with the food that everybody gives the lion.'

Calling on the lion one day, the hare told him that he was very skilled at getting lice out of lion tails.

'I can tell that you have lice in your tail,' the hare said. 'Can you not feel them itching?'

The lion thought for a moment. Now that the hare had mentioned it, he was sure that he could feel an itching in his tail.

'Remove the lice from my tail,' he roared at the hare. 'Do it right now!'

The hare smiled and said that he would set to work straight away. Quickly he went to the back of the lion and laid out his great tail on the floor. Then, taking a handful of long nails from a bag that he had with him, he hammered a nail through the lion's tail and into the floor.

The lion called out in pain and told the hare to be more careful.

'I'm sorry,' said the hare. 'These are very large lice. They are angry that I am catching them and that is why they are biting you so hard. You'll just have to put up with it until I'm finished.'

The lion grunted and lay still while the hare pretended to search for another louse. When he was ready, he took out another long nail and quickly hammered it through the lion's tail. This time the lion roared even louder.

'That was a very large louse,' the hare said. 'But don't worry, I have taken him off.'

'How many more are there?' asked the lion, his eyes watering with pain.

'Three,' replied the hare. 'And all of them seem to be very large.'

Each of the last three lice seemed more and more painful to the lion, and he howled more loudly each time the hare drove another nail into the floor. Finally the hare was finished and he came round to face the lion. Looking him directly in the eye—in a way in which no other animal would dare—the hare calmly walked over to the place where the lion kept his food and began to help himself.

The lion was so astonished at the hare's cheek that at first he did nothing. Then, roaring with rage, he tried to leap to his feet, only to be wrenched back painfully by his nailed tail.

'Release me at once!' he roared at the hare. But the other just laughed, and ate more of the lion's food. Then, when he had eaten enough, he sauntered over to another part of the lion's house and found a large knife. The lion watched him suspiciously, and tried to swipe at him with his claws, but he could barely move now and it was easy for Hare to get round him. Deftly waving his knife, Hare split the lion's skin from one end to the other and pushed him out of it. Once he was out of his skin, Lion was just a weak jelly, with no claws and no teeth. Hare pushed him aside and straight away began to free the tail of the now empty lion skin. Once he had finished this task, he slipped into the skin and bounded out of the house.

*   *   *

The baboons were frightened when they saw what they thought was the lion. Carefully they laid out a great deal of food so that the lion would eat it and not bother them. Inside the lion skin, the hare smiled to himself and cheerfully began to eat the food. When he had finished, he lay out on the ground and relaxed his lion claws. It would be pleasant to sleep in comfort in that place and wait for the baboons to bring him more food in the evening.

The next day, since the hare was eating so much food, the baboons had to travel far afield to find food for their store caves. The hare stayed put, and when his hosts had gone he slipped out of the lion skin to play with the baboon children. They enjoyed their games, with the hare chasing them in circles and the baboon children trying to catch him by his ears. Just before the baboon parents came back, however, hare got into the lion skin and was a lion again. The baboons had found a great deal of food but he managed to eat up most of it and told them that they would have to go out again the next day to find more.

That night, the baboon children told their parents that the lion was not really a lion but a hare dressed up as one. The parents did not believe them, and warned them not to say such things. One baboon, though, was suspicious, and he decided to hide the next day and see what really happened when the adult baboons had gone in search of food.

Of course the hare slipped out of his skin again and enjoyed more games with the baboon children. This was watched from a bush by the hidden baboon, whose eyes glowed with anger as he saw the deception which he and his friends had suffered at the hands of the wily hare.

'That lion is not a lion,' the baboon whispered to the others when they returned. 'The children were telling the truth—he is really a hare.'

'I see,' said the leader of the baboons. 'We shall have to drive him away.'

Taking a large stick, the head baboon went up to the sleeping lion and hit him firmly on the nose. This woke up the hare, who felt the sharp blow to his nose and howled with pain.

'That is not the sort of noise that a lion makes,' said the baboon. And with that he beat the hare again, putting all his strength into the strokes. Had the lion been a real lion, of course, that would have been the end of that baboon, but it was really only a hare and a frightened hare at that. Leaping out of the skin, he ran off into the bush, to be pursued by the angry shouts of the baboons.

The baboons took the empty lion skin back to the real lion, who was still just a weak pink thing without his claws and mane. He was grateful to be able to get into his skin, and promised that he would not trouble those baboons again. This made the baboons happy, and they decided that although they still felt angry at the way the hare had tricked them out of food, some good had come of it and they would forgive him after all.

Pumpkin

A family who lived near a river had good fields. Because they were near the river, there was never any shortage of water, even when other parts of the country were dry and dusty. There was no father in this family—he had gone off to a town and had never come back— and so the mother lived with her five sons and with her own mother and father. Although she sometimes wished that her husband would return, she knew that this would never happen, and so she reminded herself of her good fortune in having such good fields and such brave sons to look after her.

This family ate nothing but pumpkins. From the time when they had first come to that place, they had known that the ground was good for pumpkins. If you planted pumpkin seeds there, in a few months there would be large plants growing across the ground and, a few months after that, there would be great yellow pumpkins ripening in the sun. These pumpkins tasted very good. Their flesh was firm and sweet and would fill even the hungriest stomach. As the boys grew up, the woman saw that pumpkin was undoubtedly the best sort of food for a boy, as her sons were strong and took great pleasure in helping their mother in the fields.

Soon this family was known throughout that part of the country for their good pumpkins. People would walk from a great distance to buy spare pumpkins, and later they would tell their friends just how delicious these pumpkins were. The family planted more pumpkins, and soon they had so many in their fields that they were able to sell almost half of their crop, while keeping the rest for themselves.

One morning, the youngest boy, Sipho, went from the huts to fetch water at the river to water the pumpkins. He did not get as far as the river, though, as what he saw in the fields made him turn straight back. Calling out to his mother, he ran up to her hut and told her what he had seen.

The woman lost no time in running down to the fields. When she reached the first of the fences she let out a wail of sorrow.

'Our pumpkins!' she sobbed. 'Who has eaten our pumpkins?'

The other boys and the grandfather were soon in the fields as well. They looked about them and saw that many of the pumpkins had been ripped from their vines and were lying, half-eaten, on the ground. Other pumpkins had been crushed, and the seeds were scattered all over the ground. Every field looked as if it had been a battleground, with the yellow blood of the pumpkins on every stone.

The whole family set to work in clearing up the broken pumpkins. Then, when this was done, they set to repairing the fences which had been broken by whomever had done the damage. That night, the two elder boys crouched in a bush near the furthest field, waiting to see if anything would come back to wreak further havoc.

Many hours passed, but at last they heard a sound. They knew immediately what it was that had done so much damage to their crop. Of course, they were too frightened to move, and had to sit in their bush while the great elephants ate as many pumpkins as they could manage and destroyed many more. Then, when the elephants had walked away, the two boys ran to their home and told their weeping mother what they had seen.

The next day the family discussed what could be done to save their remaining pumpkins.

'There is nothing we can do,' said the grandfather, who was very old and had seen many times the damage that elephants could do. 'When elephants come to a place the only thing that people can do is to move somewhere else.'

'But we cannot leave this place,' said the mother. 'We cannot leave our beautiful fields and the good water in the river.'

'Then we shall all starve,' said the grandfather. 'The elephants will eat all our pumpkins and there shall be none left for us.'

Nobody spoke for a while. They all knew that what the grandfather had said was probably true. Then the oldest boy stood up.

'I know of a way to save our pumpkins,' he said. 'It is the only way.'

The other boys looked at him as he spoke. This boy always had the best ideas, but they wondered how even he could deal with such great beasts as elephants.

'We shall put a boy in a pumpkin,' he said. 'We shall hollow out the biggest pumpkin that we can find and we shall put a small boy inside. Then, when the elephants come back to the fields, they will be unable to resist such a good-looking pumpkin. The biggest elephant will eat it, and when the boy is inside the elephant's stomach he can strike at its heart with his knife. That will surely drive the elephants away.'

Everybody agreed that this was the best plan that could be suggested.

'You will have to get inside the pumpkin,' the oldest boy said to his youngest brother. 'You are the smallest.'

The small boy was unhappy about this plan, but since the whole family had agreed on it, he could not refuse to play his part. While the older boys went off to the fields to look for the biggest pumpkin, the mother made a special meal for her youngest son. Then she covered him with fat and gave him some special charms that she had kept for such a time.

The other boys came back to the house with the largest pumpkin that the family had seen that year. They set it on a low rock and cut a hole in its side. Then, with wooden scoops and knives, they took out the pumpkin flesh and put it in a cooking pot. Soon the pumpkin was quite hollow and they were able to push the youngest boy inside it.

It was now getting dark, and so they carried the great pumpkin down to one of the fields and placed it in the middle. No elephant could fail to spot such a delicious-looking pumpkin.

'Do not be afraid,' they said to their young brother. 'There is nothing that can go wrong with this plan.'

Inside the pumpkin, the small boy stayed quite still. If he moved, he thought it possible that an elephant would become suspicious. He had a long time to wait, and it was cramped inside the pumpkin, but, like all his brothers, this boy was brave.

*   *   *

Some hours passed before he heard the first sounds of the elephants. To begin with there was only a faint rumble, and then the whole earth seemed to shake as the elephants entered the field. The largest of the elephants, who was also their leader, looked about the field as he wondered which pumpkin to eat first. When he saw the big pumpkin in the middle, he knew immediately that that would be the best pumpkin to eat. He went across to it, sniffed at it briefly with his trunk, and then scooped it up into the air and straight into his mouth.

Inside the pumpkin, it seemed to the boy as if the whole world was turning upside down. He felt the hot breath of the elephant as the trunk embraced his pumpkin and then he sensed the sides of the pumpkin squeezing as the vegetable passed down into the great creature's throat. When the movement stopped, he realized that he was now inside the elephant's stomach. This was the time for him to cut his way out of the pumpkin and find the elephant's heart.

His knife in his hand, the boy groped his way out of the pumpkin. With a quick lunge, he struck his knife into the heart of the elephant, and then fell to his knees as the great beast roared out and lurched upon his feet.

By the time that the family arrived, the other elephants had all run away in fright. Alone in the middle of the pumpkin field, the great elephant lay on his side. The boys cut through the thick elephant skin to rescue their small brother. The mother kissed him when he emerged from within the elephant, and then she wiped away the fat and the pieces of pumpkin that stuck to his skin.

The following night, many people came to see that family to help them eat the elephant meat. They ate many pumpkins too.

Sister Of Bones

A family who lived in a dry place had two daughters. It would have been better for them to have had more girls, as there was a lot of work for women to do there. In the mornings there was cooking to do for the breakfast. Then, as the sun rose higher, there was maize to pound into powder and the yard to sweep. There were also other people's children to look after.

The hardest work, though, was the collecting of water. In the rain season there was a spring nearby which gave good, clear water for everybody to drink, but when it was dry, as it often was, the only place where water could be found was in a river a long way off. To reach the river, people had to leave in the early morning and they would only be back at midday.

It was not easy carrying calabashes of water back from the river. The sun was hot in the sky above and a dry wind came from the hills. Often the only companions along the path would be the lizards scurrying off in the dust or the cicadas screeching in the bush.

For many years it had been the task of the

first girl to go to the river for water. The second girl was not nearly as strong as her sister. Her arms were thin and it was difficult for her to walk long distances. When she was asked to carry anything, the load felt twice as heavy to her as it did to her stronger sister. For this reason, most of her work was at home, plucking chickens or doing other things which required little strength.

The mother and father of that family had spoken to many people about what was wrong with that girl. They had taken her to a witchdoctor, who had pinched her thin arms and rubbed a thick paste on them.

'That will make them strong,' he had said.

They kept the paste on the arms until it had all rubbed off, but the second girl's arms remained thin.

'She will always be weak,' her mother said to her father. 'We must accept that she is a weak girl.'

The second girl felt sad that she was not as strong as the first girl, but she did not complain. There was plenty of work even for weak girls in that dry place.

*   *   *

The first girl always fetched her water from the same spot. There was a pool in the river there, and a path that led straight down to the edge of the water. It was a place where animals came to drink, and each morning she could tell from the footprints which animals had been there before her. She could tell the marks of the leopards—who always drank at night—and the tiny marks of the duiker, who came shyly down to the river just as the sun was rising.

Every day the first girl would dip her calabashes into the pool and draw out the cool river water. Then, with the calabashes full, she would dip her hand into the pool and take up a few mouthfuls of water before she began the long journey home.

One day she felt very tired when she arrived at the river's edge. It had been especially hot that day, and it seemed to her that all her strength had been drained by the long walk. As she leaned forward to fill her calabashes, the first girl felt her head spinning around. She tried to stand up again, but she could not and slowly she tumbled forward into the water.

The river was deep and the first girl could not swim. For a few moments she struggled to get back to the edge of the pool, but there was a current in the water and it tugged at her limbs. Soon she was out in the middle of the river and it was there that she sank, with nobody to see her or to hear her last cry. Only some timid monkeys in a tree by the edge of the river saw the first girl disappear. For a few minutes they stared at the ripples in the water where she had been and then they turned away and were gone.

*   *   *

When the first girl had not returned by sunset, the father knew that something had happened to her. There was nothing he could do during the night, as there were lions nearby, but the next morning all the men went out to search for the first girl. They followed her footprints, which were clear on the ground, and traced her steps to the edge of the water. When they saw that the steps did not come back from the river's side, they cried out in sorrow, for they knew now what had happened to the first girl.

There was great sadness in that home. Everybody had loved the first girl, who had always smiled and been happy in her work. The second girl slept alone in her hut, sadly staring at the emptiness where the first girl had had her sleeping mat.

Now there was no choice but for the second girl to fetch the water each day. She set off before dawn the next morning, her heart full of sadness, wondering whether she would ever be able to carry the calabashes all the way back from the river. It was only after stopping many times that she managed her task, and when she had returned she felt as if she would never be able to walk again. Of course she knew that

38

when the next morning came she would have to set out again, and that this task would have to be performed every day until the rains came again.

For three days the second girl fetched water from the river, and each day it became harder and harder. On the fourth day, when she reached the edge of the river she dropped her calabashes on the ground and sang the song that she had made for her sister. In this song, she told how her sister had come to the river and fallen in.

In that river there were many crocodiles. They would lie out on sandbanks or float just below the surface of the water, carefully watching the animals that came to the river to drink. When they heard this song, the crocodiles slipped into the river and quietly swam closer so that they could hear the words more clearly. It was a sad song and even the crocodiles felt sorry for her.

After the song was finished, the second girl sat at the river's edge, waiting for the return of what little strength she had. The crocodiles, though, swam away into the middle of the river, to the place where the first girl had drowned. Then, diving down to the bottom of the river, they gathered the bones of the first girl and took them to a special rock they knew on the other side of the river. There they put the bones together again and made them into a girl again. They carried this girl back to where the second girl was sitting and left her there.

When the second girl saw that her sister had come back, she cried out in joy and kissed her.

'I shall carry your water,' the first girl said, 'I am stronger.'

The first girl carried the calabashes almost all the way back, but just before the village she had to stop and allow the second girl to carry them in.

'The crocodiles will not want me to leave the river now,' she said. 'I must go back.'

*   *   *

From that day onwards, whenever the second girl reached the river the first girl would be there waiting for her. After the calabashes had been filled, she would put them on her head and shoulders and carry them back for the second girl, singing all the while and telling her sister stories of what happened in the river. The second girl was happy to have her sister back and was happy too that everybody now thought that she was strong. She tried to tell her mother and father that she was helped by the first girl, but they cried out in anger that her sister was dead.

'She is not,' the second girl said quietly. 'Come with me to the river tomorrow and you shall see.'

The parents went with the second girl the next day and were happy when they saw the first girl waiting by the bank. In gratitude to the crocodiles, the father put out some meat on a rock where he knew that crocodiles liked to sit. The crocodiles smelled the meat and swallowed it quickly in their great jaws. Then they went back to some other rocks and watched the family in all its happiness.

Milk Bird

A man who had two clever children—a boy and a girl—used to go to a place where he knew were succulent wild fruits to be picked. This man knew a great deal about fruits, and he was always able to distinguish between those which were good to eat and those which were bitter in the mouth. His family, who all liked these fruits, used to wait to meet him in the evening and enjoy the food which he brought back from that special place.

It was while the man was gathering fruits that he saw a most unusual bird. There were many birds in the fruit place, as they liked to eat the seeds which the fruits produced. Many of the birds in that part were bloated from the goodness of their food, and could not fly as high or as quickly as other birds. For this reason, if anybody wanted to catch a bird, then that was the easiest place for it to be done.

The unusual bird was standing in the grass, his head barely showing. If the man had not been looking in that direction, he would have missed him, but, as it happened, his eyes alighted on the bird's head and he drew in his breath in astonishment.

On the top of the bird's head there was a plume of feathers. These feathers were not grey, as were the feathers on top of the snake-eating birds, but were coloured red and green. The neck, which could just be made out, was white.

The man watched the bird, which had not seen him and was showing no sign of fear. After a moment or two, the bird strutted forward a few paces, and so the man was able to see more of its body. He saw now that the belly was covered with red feathers and those on the bird's long legs were white and black. The bird moved its head, as if looking for something, and took a few more steps.

The man watched the bird for a few moments. There was a great deal of fruit that had ripened that day, but he found that he could think only of the bird and of how he would like to take the bird home. He was worried that if he approached the bird, it would take to the air and disappear, but he knew that if he did nothing he would never be able to forget that he had lost the chance of capturing the most beautiful of all birds.

The man crept forward, taking care not to allow his footsteps to be heard. There were twigs on the ground, and large stones, but he avoided these carefully and was soon only a short distance away from his quarry. Then, with a great lunge, he flung himself on top of the bird and pinned it to the ground.

To the man's surprise, the bird did not struggle. As it lay beneath him, its wings and its body immobile, it merely looked up at him with its dark eyes, and blinked.

The man took out his fruit bag and slipped the bird into it. Then, deciding not to bother to gather any more fruit, he turned round and made for home as quickly as he could. He could not wait to see the surprise of his children when they saw the marvellous bird which he had found.

*   *   *

When he arrived home, it was almost dark and the children had gone into their huts. The man sat at his wife's side and told her of the bird he had found.

'It is a most unusual bird,' he explained. 'There are many people who would like to have a bird like this one.'

The woman asked him to open his bag, and he did so, making sure that the bird was unable to fly out of the open neck of the bag. The woman looked in and let out a cry of surprise.

'I have heard of that sort of bird before,' she said. 'That is the sort of bird which gives milk.'

The man was most surprised that his wife should have heard of so unusual a bird, but he knew that her father had been a man who knew the names of all the birds and that she must have obtained her knowledge from him. Carefully reaching into the bag, he took the bird out and held it before his wife. She quickly fetched a calabash and began to milk the bird. After only a few moments, the calabash was full with sweet-smelling milk, which the man and the woman both drank. Then they put the bird into a spare hut which they had and closed the door.

The next morning the woman went into the hut and, after waiting a few moments for her eyes to become accustomed to the darkness, she sought out the bird and milked it again. Then she took the calabash of milk to her children, who drank it all and asked for more.

'You may have more tonight,' she said. 'From now on, there will always be such milk for you.'

*   *   *

The children were delighted with the fresh supply of such delicious milk. Every morning they drank their fill, and their parents finished off the rest. With all the milk they were getting, the children began to grow larger and sleeker, and their skin shone with good health.

At the end of a month, the children began to be inquisitive about the source of the milk.

'I don't understand how we get such sweet milk from our cows,' the girl said to her mother. 'They have never given such milk before.'

The woman smiled, and said nothing.

'Perhaps you have a secret cow somewhere,' suggested the boy.

Once again the mother said nothing. She did not want to tell her children that what they were drinking was bird's milk, as she had heard from her father that children did not like to think they were drinking milk from birds. If they stopped drinking the milk, then they would surely lose all the fat which they had put on and which made them so much admired by everybody else in that place.

*　　　　*　　　　*

The girl went to her brother that evening and said that she had a plan. The next day, they would put a small bowl of the milk outside and wait to see which animals came to drink it. In this way they would know where the milk came from and their curiosity would be satisfied.

When their mother gave them the calabash the next day, the girl poured a little of the milk into a bowl and gave it to her brother. He slipped out of the hut and put the bowl down at the edge of the bush. Then the two of them watched, waiting for the first animal to drink the milk.

A hyena walked past, sniffed at the milk, but

did not drink it. Then there came a baboon, who peered into the bowl, but did not touch the milk. The baboon was followed by a rock rabbit, which also showed no sign of wanting to drink the milk. At long last, a bird landed near the bowl, and soon had his beak dipped in the milk. After him there came more birds, until the bowl could not be seen for the fluttering of wings about it.

'That is bird's milk we have been drinking,' the boy said. 'Now we know.'

*   *   *

The children were keen to see the bird from which their parents were obtaining the milk, and so they hid in a place where they could watch their mother as she came out of her hut in the morning. They both saw her go to the empty hut and look about her before she opened the door. Then they saw her come out again with the calabash in her hand and they knew immediately that the bird was being kept in that hut.

'We shall go and see the bird when our parents are in the fields,' the boy said. 'I have heard that birds which give milk are very colourful.'

That afternoon, as the man and the woman were in the fields, the two children crept up to the bird's hut and opened the door. Once inside, they looked about nervously and it was a few minutes before they saw the bird sitting in his corner. The bird watched them suspiciously. He had grown used to the man and his wife, but the children were unfamiliar.

The children approached the bird and looked closely at him, while the bird stared back with its dark eyes, and blinked.

The boy looked at the bird's feathers and shook his head.

'It is sad,' he said. 'The bird has lost all the colour from his feathers.'

When it heard this, the bird looked down at his own feathers and sighed.

'It is because I have been kept in here for so long,' the bird said to the boy. 'I have not seen the sun for many weeks.'

The boy shook his head.

'I am sorry,' he said.

'If that is so,' said the bird, 'you should take me out into the sunshine for a few minutes. A short time in the open air would restore all the colours to my feathers.'

The boy and the girl agreed to do this for the bird. Carefully they lifted him in their arms and took him out into the open. Then they set him down on a low branch of a tree and watched the colour return to his feathers. It happened quite quickly, and soon the bird was no longer faded.

'He is looking happier,' the girl whispered to

her brother. 'His feathers are normal again.'

'Thank you,' said the bird. And with that, he flew up into the air and had soon disappeared. The girl looked at the boy and wailed.

'We shall never be forgiven,' she said. 'We shall never find a bird like that again.'

*   *   *

The boy was frightened of telling his father what had happened, and so he went out into the hills to look for another bird which was exactly the same as the bird which had escaped. He searched in all the places he knew birds liked, but in none of these did he find a bird which looked at all similar. On his way home, though, he was surprised by a strange sound in the grass. There, sheltering behind a small bush, was a bird which looked almost the same as the milk bird. The boy seized the bird, which did not resist but just looked at him, and blinked.

That night the woman went to milk the bird in its special hut. After she had finished, she brought the calabash out and gave it to her husband. He raised it to his lips and took a sip.

'This is not milk,' he said. 'It is water. Why has our bird given us only water?'

The woman was unable to answer his question. She went back to the bird and tried again to milk it, but once more all that the bird gave was water. This made the woman wail, as she could think of no reason why the bird should suddenly have turned against them in this way.

The next day, while their parents sat under a tree and mourned the change in their bird, the two children crept out into the bush to see if they could find another bird that would give milk. They felt responsible for the loss of the first bird, and they knew that sooner or later they would have to confess to their parents what had really happened. They walked far, and eventually they came to a place where there was a group of boys calling out in excitement. They ran over to join the group of boys and saw that they had surrounded a bird and were throwing stones at it and calling it names.

The boy and his sister were angered at the cruelty of the boys. They seized two large sticks which were nearby and drove the other boys away, telling them that it was wrong to surround such a bird and torment it. Then they looked at the bird, which was lying on the ground, its breast trembling with fear. At once they knew it was the milk bird.

Gently, the boy lifted up the milk bird and carried it home. Without being seen by the parents, he took the bird into the hut and exchanged it for the water bird. The water bird then flew away, cackling with pleasure at

51

its freedom.

The milk bird did not attempt to escape again. It was grateful to the boy and his sister and from that time on gave milk which was sweeter than ever before. The milk bird stayed alive until the boy and his sister grew up and left that place. Then it fell to the floor of its dark hut, its heart broken with sorrow.

Beware Of Friends You Cannot Trust

Hyena was miserable. It was some time since he had eaten, and there was no food to be seen anywhere. He sat by the side of the road and tried to remember his last meal, but all he could think of was the pain that was gnawing away at his stomach.

As Hyena sat in misery, Jackal walked past. He was never miserable, as he always had enough to eat. He looked at hyena and asked him why he was so downcast.

'It is because I have had no food for days,' Hyena howled. 'Other animals are fat and sleek, but I am just bones. It might be better if I were to die now, rather than to wait.'

'Well your troubles are over, Uncle,' said Jackal. 'It happens that I know a very good place for food.'

'Will you show it to me?' asked Hyena. 'I only want a little.'

'I will do that with pleasure,' said Jackal, preening himself as he spoke. 'All you have to do is follow me.'

The two friends made their way to a place which Jackal knew. It was a place where men lived, and it had a stock pen around which the men had built a high fence.

'This is the place,' said Jackal. 'That pen is full of sheep and goats. We can eat as much as we like.'

'But what about the fence?' asked Hyena. 'It is far too high for us to jump over.'

Jackal smirked. 'I have a way in,' he said confidently.

'There is a hole in that fence. It is only a small hole, but we shall be able to squeeze through it.'

Hyena followed Jackal to the place where the hole was. As Jackal had said, it was not a big hole, but they both just managed to get through and found themselves standing in the animal pen. And Jackal had been right. There were many sheep and goats standing about, peering at the two unwelcome visitors, waiting to be eaten.

'Do not eat the goats,' Jackal whispered. 'They make a great noise and will wake the men. Eat only the sheep.'

The two friends then chased some sheep into a corner.

'You eat the fat one,' said Jackal. 'I will eat the small one.'

Hyena though that this was most generous of Jackal, as had he been in Jackal's position he would undoubtedly have chosen to eat the fat sheep.

The sheep tasted good. Hyena ate and ate

until he had eventually finished even the bones and skin of the fat sheep. Jackal finished his sheep more quickly, as it was much smaller.

Then they prepared to leave. As he stood up, Hyena felt his belly sag beneath him. It had been a very long time since he had had such a large amount to eat and his skin was stretched thin to accommodate all the delicious meat.

'I will just take one bite out of a goat,' Jackal announced. 'Goat meat is very delicious and it would help the rest of my meal go down.'

No sooner had he said this, than he pounced on a goat and took a bite out of its leg. The goat cried out and made a terrible bleating noise. This awoke the dogs who were sleeping near the huts. They barked furiously and in due course awoke the men.

'We shall have to leave quickly,' said Jackal, darting for the hole by which they had entered.

Jackal slipped out of the hole without difficulty, but when it came to Hyena's turn he was so round from eating the fat sheep that he could not get through. He struggled and wriggled, but it was no good. Soon the people were upon him, beating him with their knobkerries and shouting angry words at him. By the time he managed to escape, he was covered with dreadful bruises.

Hyena went off to a quiet place and wept. He had now forgotten the delicious meal which he had enjoyed and all that remained was the burning pain from the blows which the people had inflicted on him. Hyena wept many tears. Some were for the shame of what had been done to him; others were over friends who could not be trusted.

Children Of Wax

Not far from the hills of the Matopos there lived a family whose children were made out of wax. The mother and the father in this family were exactly the same as everyone else, but for some reason their children had turned out to be made of wax. At first this caused them great sorrow, and they wondered who had put such a spell on them, but later they became quite accustomed to this state of affairs and grew to love their children dearly.

It was easy for the parents to love the wax children. While other children might fight among themselves or forget to do their duty, wax children were always dutiful and never fought with one another. They were also hard workers, one wax child being able to do the work of at least two ordinary children.

The only real problem which the wax children gave was that people had to avoid making fires too close to them, and of course they also had to work only at night. If they worked during the day, when the sun was hot, wax children would melt.

To keep them out of the sun, their father made the wax children a dark hut that had no windows. During the day no rays of the sun could penetrate into the gloom of this hut, and so the wax children were quite safe. Then, when the sun had gone down, the children would come out of their dark hut and begin their work. They tended the crops and watched over the cattle, just as ordinary children did during the daytime.

There was one wax child, Ngwabi, who used to talk about what it was like during the day.

'We can never know what the world is like,' he said to his brothers and sisters. 'When we come out of our hut everything is quite dark and we see so little.'

Ngwabi's brothers and sisters knew that what he said was right, but they accepted they would never know what the world looked like. There were other things that they had which the other children did not have, and they contented themselves with these. They knew, for instance, that other children felt pain: wax children never experienced pain, and for this they were grateful.

But poor Ngwabi still longed to see the world. In his dreams he saw the hills in the distance and watched the clouds that brought rain. He saw paths that led this way and that through the bush, and he longed to be able to follow them. But that was something that a wax child could never do, as it was far too dangerous to follow such paths in the night-time.

As he grew older, this desire of Ngwabi's to see what the world was really like when the sun was up grew stronger and stronger. At last he was unable to contain it any more and he ran out of the hut one day when the sun was riding high in the sky and all about there was light and more light. The other children screamed, and some of them tried to grab at him as he left the hut, but they failed to stop their brother and he was gone.

Of course he could not last long in such heat. The sun burned down on Ngwabi and before he had taken more than a few steps he felt all the strength drain from his limbs. Crying out to his brothers and sisters, he fell to the ground and was soon nothing more than a pool of wax in the dust. Inside the hut, afraid to leave its darkness, the other wax children wept for their melted brother.

When night came, the children left their hut and went to the spot where Ngwabi had fallen. Picking up the wax, they went to a special place they knew and there Ngwabi's eldest sister made the wax into a bird. It was a bird with great wings and for feathers they put a covering of leaves from the trees that grew there. These leaves would protect the wax from the sun so that it would not melt when it became day.

After they had finished their task, they told

59

their parents what had happened. The man and woman wept, and each of them kissed the wax model of a bird. Then they set it upon a rock that stood before the wax children's hut.

The wax children did not work that night. At dawn they were all in their hut, peering through a small crack that there was in the wall. As the light came up over the hills, it made the wax bird seem pink with fire. Then, as the sun itself rose over the fields, the great bird which they had made suddenly moved its wings and launched itself into the air. Soon it was high above the ground, circling over the children's hut. A few minutes later it was gone, and the children knew that their brother was happy at last.

Brave Hunter

There were many brave hunters in those days, but there was only one of them who *liked* danger. Other hunters faced up to danger when they went hunting, but did not go out of their way to find it. This man was different: it would have been easy for him to hunt in the flat land, where there were wide skies and light, but he chose instead to go into dark and thick forests. There he met leopards, snakes and some creatures that were half animal, half person and very dangerous. None of these creatures frightened this brave hunter, who would come home and tell people of what he had seen. As they listened to his stories, everybody knew that this was a hunter whose heart was stronger and harder than any other's in that part of the country.

This hunter married a girl who was soon expecting his child. All the people who knew her were looking forward to the day when the child was due to be born, as they knew that it would be a most unusual child. If it was a boy, then it would be as brave as its father; if it was a girl, then it would be more beautiful than any other children. The woman knew this too, and she faced each day with the smile of one who realizes that she is worthy of her brave husband.

The hunter was overjoyed when his wife gave birth to a strong boy. He heard the child crying lustily from the birthing hut and he gave a leap of delight when he recognized the cry as the cry of a male child.

'A small hunter is born,' he said to his friends.

And they nodded and said: 'He will be very brave—just like you.'

So proud was the father of his child that he decided that the naming ceremony would be one which would be remembered by people for many years. For this reason, he announced to all his friends that at the ceremony he would take the life of a leopard cub, as a sacrifice for the future of his young son.

The hunter's friends were astonished at this claim. They all knew that to take a leopard cub from its mother was the most dangerous thing that any man could do. At the same time, they realized that if anybody could do such a thing, then it would be this brave hunter.

*　　　*　　　*

The hunter chose the darkest and most dangerous forest for the place where he would find the leopard cub for sacrifice. He showed no fear as he wandered into this forest, and paid no attention to the whispering sounds and the cracking of twigs which were all about him. Soon he found a place that smelled strongly of leopard and there, in a small clearing, were two leopard cubs, sleeping up against one another for comfort and warmth. Before the cubs could run away, the hunter swooped upon them and carried the little creatures out of the forest. It was a very brave thing to do, but a thing that only a man with a heart as hard as his would have done.

The people who saw him return with the two baby leopards were filled with excitement. They talked of nothing else and made special beer for the brave hunter to drink while he told them of how he had found the cubs in the darkest part of the darkest forest.

*   *   *

When the leopard mother returned, she called her children, but received no answer. She searched through the forest for them, looking under all the trees and bushes and into all the secret forest places which leopards like to lie in. The more she called, the emptier the forest seemed, and slowly she came to understand that her cubs had been taken away. When she saw the tracks that the hunter had made as he left the forest, she knew in her heart that a terrible thing had happened to her children and she cried deep tears for the cubs she had loved so much.

Her eyes full of these tears, the leopard mother followed the tracks back towards the village. As she came closer to the place where the people lived, she slowly changed herself into a beautiful woman. By the time she reached the hunter's house she was one of the most beautiful women who had ever walked past that place.

When the hunter looked out of his hut and saw a beautiful woman standing in front of it, he called out in his brave voice:

'What are you doing in front of my house?'

The leopard mother looked into the darkness of the hut and said:

'I am a stranger and I have no place to sleep tonight. I am frightened that I shall be in danger because I am not nearly as brave as you are.'

These words pleased the hunter, who shouted out to her that she could spend that night in his hut. The leopard mother said that she was very grateful to him for his kindness and she entered the hut and lay down upon the floor.

As darkness fell, the leopard mother asked the hunter what he was going to be doing the next day.

'It is the naming ceremony of my young son,'

he said proudly. 'I shall be sacrificing two baby leopards to mark the special occasion. My son shall have the skins to sleep upon when he is ready to leave his mother.'

The leopard mother looked up at the brave hunter and begged him to spare the lives of the two cubs.

'They are only leopards,' she said. 'But please be generous to them and let them live. Think how sad their mother will be.'

The hunter laughed at the suggestion which came from this beautiful woman and replied that it would be impossible for him to change his mind. He had already announced to the whole village that the cubs would be sacrificed and they would not think him brave if he changed his mind.

On hearing this, the leopard mother wept bitterly, but the hunter just watched as the beautiful woman sobbed on his floor. When she continued to weep, he lay back on his bed and told her that she should go outside and only come back when her crying had finished.

'Why weep for two leopards?' he asked. 'They are not worth weeping over.'

As he spoke, he suddenly saw that the beautiful woman on his floor was changing into a leopard. He tried to rise to his feet, but he was not quick enough. Before he could reach for his spear, the leopard mother was upon him, her sharp claws uncurled, her sleek ears swept back in anger. The brave hunter screamed, but nobody heard him.

*   *   *

The next morning the people waited outside his hut for the naming ceremony to begin and wondered why no sounds came from within. They could not see, of course, the leopard mother playing with her cubs in the forest, nor hear them singing their leopard songs in the darkness.

Stone Hare

It was a time when there was a great shortage of water. Throughout the country the waterholes had dried up, leaving only parched expanses of baked mud. Only one waterhole remained, and in that there was very little water.

The lion was so concerned about the problem that he called the animals together to discuss it.

'The only thing we can do is to take turns,' he said. 'If we each have only one drink a day, the waterhole will last until the rains come.'

The animals all nodded at the wisdom of this suggestion and they agreed that this is what they would have to do. Even the hare agreed.

As the days passed, the system which the lion had suggested worked well. The shyer creatures would go to the waterhole early in the morning, drink a few sips of water, and then move away. As the morning wore on, the other animals would come to the water's edge, drink just enough to keep them going for a day, and then go back to their search. The lion himself, who had a large belly which needed a great deal of water, took only a few mouthfuls and then walked away.

Hare, though, began to wonder why he was bothering to keep the promise he had made. Eventually one evening he went to the waterhole for a second visit. There was nobody about and he was able to plunge into the water and drink to his heart's delight. Then, when his thirst was quenched, he swam about in the remaining water, washing all the dust and dirt out of his fur.

When he got out, Hare looked back and saw that the water was badly muddied from where he had been cavorting. This worried him, as he knew that when the lion came for his drink the next day he would be very angry. Hare thought for a moment, and then he had an idea of how he would deal with this problem.

Picking up some mud in his paws, he quietly made his way to the place where he knew the hyena would sleep at night. Then, creeping up to the hyena, he smeared the mud all over the sleeping creature's legs. As he did so, he smiled with pleasure at the thought of his cleverness, realizing what would happen to the hyena the following day.

As Hare had imagined, Lion was furious when he was told that the water remaining in the hole had been stolen and muddied. He went round each of the animals and asked them if they knew who could have done such a treacherous thing. When Hare was asked, he responded quickly.

'I saw the hyena do it,' he said. 'I saw him last night—drinking the water and then swimming in it.'

'Do you have any proof?' asked Lion.

'Look at his legs,' Hare replied simply. 'You will find your proof there.'

*　　　*　　　*

Lion lost no time in seeking out the hyena. When he saw the mud on his legs, he roared in anger and asked Hyena why he had behaved in so selfish a manner.

'I do not understand what you are saying,' the hyena replied.

This answer served only to enrage Lion further. With another roar, he bounded over to Hyena and killed him with one swipe. Hyena fell to the ground and was immediately divided into four pieces by Lion. Then Lion called the other animals to assist him in carrying Hyena to a place where they would be able to cook him for a feast. Hare was given a heavy piece and as he carried it along he sang under his breath a song which told all about a clever hare who had fooled a stupid lion.

One of the other animals heard snatches of this song and asked hare what it was about. Hare replied with a lie, but continued to sing about the doings of the clever hare, who was no longer thirsty and had clean fur.

Unfortunately for Hare, Lion's acute hearing enabled him to hear the words of the song. Lion dropped the piece of Hyena that he was carrying and began to chase Hare, warning him that he was about to join Hyena at the feast—but not as a guest!

Hare ran ahead of Lion but soon found himself trapped by a deep ravine. He had no way of escaping other than by turning himself into a smooth stone, which he did.

Lion stopped at the edge of the ravine and looked about him in puzzlement. He roared once or twice to see if he could frighten Hare into giving away his hiding place, but he did not succeed. Angry at the way in which he had been outwitted by this tricky creature, he picked up the smooth stone that lay at his feet and hurled it across to the other side of the ravine.

Hare sailed through the air, landing softly in the thick grass that grew on the other side of the ravine. Then, almost immediately, he changed himself back into a hare and called out in mockery to the lion.

Lion was angrier that ever before, but he was unable to do anything about his anger. The more that Lion roared, the more did Hare laugh and call out how clever he had been.

Lion realized—too late—that there were

some tricky people who could never be trusted, and that Hare was one of them.

A Tree To Sing To

This happened in a time of famine. For months there had been no rain and the sky was empty of clouds. People prayed for rain and used powerful magic to bring on the heavy purple clouds that would save the land, but all this was to no avail. The cattle became thinner and thinner as they nibbled at the last shreds of vegetation. Then, when these disappeared, there was nothing left but the dust and the cattle began to die.

But there was one man who was eating. This man, Sibanda, had found a tree which grew by the dusty bed of an empty river. It had been his shelter after a long walk in search of food and he had sat underneath it to rest before he continued on his way home. It was in a lonely place, and so Sibanda sang to make himself feel braver. Because he was hungry, the first words that came into his mind were about food, and so he sang:

I must have food. Oh, give me food!
Please give me food!

Sibanda sang these lines only once or twice

when he heard a sound in the leaves above him. Thinking it might be a snake—for mambas like to hide in such trees—he leapt to his feet and gazed into the branches of the tree.

At first the poor man thought that his eyes were deceiving him. Perhaps I've been out in the fierce sun too long, he said to himself. Perhaps it is making me dream. But when he looked again, he saw that it was no dream. The tree was beginning to shower him with food. He lifted up his hands and caught the food that came down to him. It was real and it tasted very good. Never before had he tasted such food, and he had soon eaten it all up.

That evening, Sibanda sat at his fireside and watched his wife preparing the small amount of food that would have to feed the whole family. There was very little to eat, and he knew that all the children would be going to bed hungry that night.

'Here,' said his wife. 'Take your share.'

Sibanda shook his head and passed the food on to his youngest child.

'My children must eat,' he said. 'I shall go hungry.'

Of course he was not really hungry. In fact, he had eaten so much of the food that the tree had given him that he could hardly move.

When his wife saw what her husband was doing, she was filled with admiration for him.

Here is a truly noble husband, she thought. Here is a man who will not eat when his family is hungry.

*　　　*　　　*

The following day Sibanda made his way to the dry river bed and again found the tree that had provided him with food. I shall sing to it again, he decided. I shall eat again today.

Standing underneath the tree, Sibanda raised his head and sang loudly into the wide branches above him. This time he chose different words:

> They gobble down all the food at home:
> They won't leave any for me.

When the tree heard this sorrowful song, it moved its branches as if it were weeping. Sibanda watched the movement and then, to his delight, he saw food come showering down. Quickly he gathered it all up and stuffed it into his mouth. Then he sat down, rubbing his swollen stomach, and went to sleep. He was filled with a great happiness and in his dreams he saw more and more food stretching out before him. They were the dreams of a well-fed man.

At home that evening, Sibanda once again declined the offer of food which his wife made.

'I have told you,' he said. 'I cannot eat until all my children are fat once more. I prefer to starve.'

Sibanda's wife was astonished at her husband's goodness. I always thought him an ordinary man, she reflected. Now I know that the father of my children is a great man.

*   *   *

And so it continued for many days. Each morning Sibanda would sneak off to his food tree and sing to it about the greediness of his wife and family. And the tree, feeling sorry for him, would move its boughs, although there was no wind, and it would let down all sorts of delicious food. Then, when he could eat no more, Sibanda would return to his home and would refuse to eat. Like a man suffering much because he can smell food but not touch it, he would watch his family take their miserable portion of thin soup, refusing himself to take his share.

It is possible that this might have gone on for months, had it not been for the curiosity of one of Sibanda's daughters. This girl, who had watched her father getting fatter and fatter, began to wonder how it was that a man could grow fat if he never ate. In times of drought it was usual for everyone to become thinner— indeed many feared that they might die. Yet her father, who ate nothing at all, was now the fattest man in the village.

This girl decided to follow her father. As he sneaked away one morning, she was watching him from behind a tree. Quietly, so as not to attract his attention, she followed him along the path that he took towards the river bed. When he reached the food tree, she hid herself behind a rock.

Quite unaware that one of his daughters was behind him, Sibanda reached the tree and began to sing to it:

> My family eats like hungry dogs—
> I wait at the side like a timid cat.

As usual, the tree disgorged its food, and the astonished girl watched her father eating with the speed of a man who has not eaten for many weeks. Then, when he went to sleep beneath the tree, the surprised child ran back along the path to her mother's house. There she told the story of what had happened, and her mother wept with anger when she heard of the selfishness of her husband.

The next day, when Sibanda made his secret way to the river bed, he was followed by the whole family. He did not know that they were following him, for they moved silently, like thin dogs. But when he stood beneath the tree, the woman and her children ran out shouting.

Assembling all her children beneath the branches of the tree, she sang out to the trunk and the leaves:

> A selfish man stands here:
> He eats while his family grows thin.

When it heard this, the tree gave a great shudder. For a few seconds it seemed as if it would tear itself out by its roots, but after a while it calmed down and began to shed food for the hungry family.

'You see!' shouted the embarrassed man. 'This tree has food for all of us.'

Eagerly he bent down to pick up some food, but when he put it into his mouth he spat it out quickly. He tried some more, but had to do the same thing again, for everything that the tree gave him tasted bitter in his mouth. The food that the tree gave to the woman and her children was as sweet as ever.

A Blind Man Catches A Bird

A young man married a woman whose brother was blind. The young man was eager to get to know his new brother-in-law and so he asked him if he would like to go hunting with him.

'I cannot see,' the blind man said. 'But you can help me see when we are out hunting together. We can go.'

The young man led the blind man off into the bush. At first they followed a path that he knew and it was easy for the blind man to tag on behind the other. After a while, though, they went off into thicker bush, where the trees grew closely together and there were many places for the animals to hide. The blind man now held on to the arm of his sighted brother-in-law and told him many things about the sounds that they heard around them. Because he had no sight, he had a great ability to interpret the noises made by animals in the bush.

'There are warthogs around,' he would say, 'I can hear their noises over there.'

Or: 'That bird is preparing to fly. Listen to the sound of its wings unfolding.'

To the brother-in-law, these sounds were

meaningless, and he was most impressed at the blind man's ability to understand the bush although it must have been for him one great darkness.

They walked on for several hours, until they reached a place where they could set their traps. The blind man followed the other's advice, and put his trap in a place where birds might come for water. The other man put his trap a short distance away, taking care to disguise it so that no bird would know that it was there. He did not bother to disguise the blind man's trap, as it was hot and he was eager to get home to his new wife. The blind man thought that he had disguised his trap, but he did not see that he had failed to do so and any bird could tell that there was a trap there.

They returned to their hunting place the next day. The blind man was excited at the prospect of having caught something, and the young man had to tell him to keep quiet, or he would scare all the animals away. Even before they reached the traps, the blind man was able to tell that they had caught something.

'I can hear birds,' he said. 'There are birds in the traps.'

When he reached his trap, the young man saw that he had caught a small bird. He took it out of the trap and put it in a pouch that he had brought with him. Then the two of them walked towards the blind man's trap.

'There is a bird in it,' he said to the blind man. 'You have caught a bird too.'

As he spoke, he felt himself filling with jealousy. The blind man's bird was marvellously coloured, as if it had flown through a rainbow and been stained by the colours. The feathers from a bird such as that would make a fine present for his new wife, but the blind man had a wife too, and she would also want the feathers.

The young man bent down and took the blind man's bird from the trap. Then, quickly substituting his own bird, he passed it to the blind man and put the coloured bird into his own pouch.

'Here is your bird,' he said to the blind man. 'You may put it in your pouch.'

The blind man reached out for the bird and took it. He felt it for a moment, his fingers passing over the wings and the breast. Then, without saying anything, he put the bird into his pouch and they began the trip home.

On their way home, the two men stopped to rest under a broad tree. As they sat there, they talked about many things. The young man was impressed with the wisdom of the blind man, who knew a great deal, although he could see nothing at all.

'Why do people fight with one another?' he asked the blind man. It was a question which

81

had always troubled him and he wondered if the blind man could give him an answer.

The blind man said nothing for a few moments, but it was clear to the young man that he was thinking. Then the blind man raised his head, and it seemed to the young man as if the unseeing eyes were staring right into his soul. Quietly he gave his answer.

'Men fight because they do to each other what you have just done to me.'

The words shocked the young man and made him ashamed. He tried to think of a response, but none came. Rising to his feet, he fetched his pouch, took out the brightly coloured bird and gave it back to the blind man.

The blind man took the bird, felt over it with his fingers, and smiled.

'Do you have any other questions for me?' he asked.

'Yes,' said the young man. 'How do men become friends after they have fought?'

The blind man smiled again.

'They do what you have just done,' he said. 'That's how they become friends again.'

Hare Fools Lion—Again

A woman who used to go out to cut grass for thatching once came across a place where there was a great deal of grass. There had been good rains there, and the soil was rich and nourishing. Where the rains had fallen, the grass had grown higher than any other grass she had seen, and now it waved golden brown in the wind.

The woman was overjoyed at the sight of so much thatching grass and she immediately began to cut it down with her sickle. She worked at this task all day, pausing only to wipe her forehead of the beads of moisture that sprang from the hard work she was doing. From the side of the field, a hare was watching her, thinking what a good woman she was to do all this hard work while other people were sitting about under the trees and telling long stories about the hard work that they used to do a long time ago.

Toward the end of the afternoon, when all the heat had gone out of the sun, the woman stacked up the grass she had cut and loaded it onto her back. She was a strong woman, but even for her the weight of this load was almost more than she could manage. She was determined, though, that she would carry all this grass back to her husband, and so she staggered off down the path that led back towards her house.

The woman had only walked for a short distance when she felt that she would have to put her load down.

'If I don't rest,' she said to herself, 'my back will break.'

After a short time, she again loaded the bundle of grass onto her back and began to walk again down the winding path. It was a path surrounded by dense bush, and she knew that it was a place where it was dangerous to stop too long. She was unwilling to linger long in that place, but soon she had to put her bundle down again. When she tried to load it onto her back, however, she found that she just did not have the strength to do this.

'If only somebody would help me!' she called out in her distress. 'If some strong person would help me carry this burden I should let him marry my daughter.'

As she finished speaking there was a sound from the bush beside the path and out of it there came a large lion. He was the most powerful lion that the woman had ever seen, and she wailed in fright at the sight of his great shoulders and the shock of golden mane that framed his face.

'You need the help of a lion,' the lion said to her. 'Load that grass on my back and I shall carry it back to your house.'

The woman was seized by fear, but she managed to get the bundle onto the back of the lion and together they walked down the path, the woman in front, leading the way, the lion behind, his lion breath hot against the bare skin of the woman's legs.

When the woman's husband saw his wife coming down the path, followed by a lion, he let out a great shout. All his friends, woken up by this cry, leapt to their feet and ran towards the fence of tree trunks, beating drums and shouting threats at the lion. The lion saw all these excited men, and although he was strong and brave, he decided to run away before they could throw spears into his hide. As he ran, the grass fell off his back and was quickly scraped up into a bundle by the woman.

*   *   *

Many days passed after this strange event and the woman forgot all about the lion—and the promise she had made to him. When her husband suggested that they should all make a journey to see his uncle and his uncle's children, the woman readily agreed. Together with her husband and her daughter, she set off along the path that led to the uncle's house,

85

not thinking of the fact that this path ran right past a place that was very much liked by large lions.

And indeed, there he was, waiting for them in the middle of the path, his great mane bristling, his strong shoulder muscles rippling like the surface of water in a breeze.

'So this is the daughter you promised me,' the lion said. 'She is very beautiful and I look forward to marrying her.'

The husband looked in consternation at his wife, who merely lowered her gaze to the ground and told him that what the lion said was quite true. The girl, who had never seen a lion before, wept at the thought that she would have to marry such a frightening creature.

In some thick grass at the edge of the path, the hare sat watching the difficult situation that was now developing.

'Please! Please!' he shouted, as he bounded out onto the path. 'Some help is needed!'

The lion looked at the hare and asked him why this help was needed.

'There are some rocks nearby,' said the hare. 'These rocks are about to fall. If they fall they will crush the crops that I have spent so much time growing. Please help me.'

The lion was a bit unwilling to help such a small creature, but when he saw that the others were happy to do so, he grudgingly agreed. Pleased at their willingness to help,

Hare led them through a field to a place where there were great rocks of granite, balancing on one another, as often happens in that part of the country.

'You hold there,' he said to the lion. 'Lean against the rock with all your might.'

The hare then positioned the three others underneath a rock, telling them to push against it with all their strength. Then he stood back and looked at the people supporting the balancing rocks.

'I have a very good idea,' he said after a few moments. 'If I get poles to hold up the rocks, this will be much less strain on your arms.'

The lion and the people all agreed that this was a good idea, and so the hare went up to the man and said:

'You must go to a place nearby and look for a pole called "Go for good and never come back." Take your wife with you.'

Then the hare walked up to the daughter and said to her:

'You must go to a place nearby and look for a pole called "Also go for good."'

Then he stood back and watched while the three people went off in search of these poles. After a while, he called out to the lion that he was going to find out what had happened to the people.

'They are taking a very long time to find these poles,' he said. 'Please wait here while I go to find them.'

The lion waited patiently under the rock. After several hours the others had still not returned and the next morning, when there was still no sign of any of them, he remembered the names of the poles. He was angry at being tricked and the people heard his roars from many miles away. They were safely in their houses, however, celebrating with the daughter her luck at being saved from such a frightening husband.

Strange Animal

There were many people to tell that boy what to do. There was his mother and his father, his grandfather, and his older brother. And there was also an aunt, who was always saying: 'Do this. Do that.' Every day this aunt would shout at him, and make a great noise that would frighten the birds.

The boy did not like his aunt. Sometimes he thought that he might go to some man to buy some medicine to put into her food to make her quiet, but of course he never did this. In spite of all his aunt's shouting and ordering about, the boy always obeyed her, as his father said he must.

'She has nothing to do but shout at you,' the boy's father explained. 'It keeps her happy.'

'When I'm a big man I'll come and shout in her ear,' the boy said. It was good to think about that.

There was a place that the aunt knew where a lot of fruit grew. It was a place which was quite far away, and the boy did not like going there. Near this place there were caves and the boy had heard that a strange animal lived in these caves. One of his friends had seen this strange animal and had warned people about going near that place.

But the aunt insisted on sending the boy to pick fruit there, and so he went, his heart a cold stone of fear inside him. He found the trees and began to pick the fruit, but a little later he heard the sound of something in the bush beside him. He stopped his task and stood near the tree in case the strange animal should be coming.

Out of the bush came the strange animal. It was just as his friend had described it and the boy was very frightened. Quickly he took out the drum which he had brought with him and began to beat it. The strange animal stopped, looked at the boy in surprise, and began to dance.

*   *   *

All day the boy played the drum, keeping the strange animal dancing. As long as he played the drum, he knew that there was nothing that the strange animal could do to harm him. At last, when night came, the strange animal stopped dancing and disappeared back into the bush. The boy knew that it had gone back to its cave and so he was able to walk home safely. When he reached home, though, his aunt had prepared her shouting.

'Where is all the fruit?' she shouted.

Thinking that he had eaten it, she then began to beat him until the boy was able to run away from her and hide in his own hut.

The boy told his father the next day of the real reason why he had been unable to bring back fruit from the tree. He explained that there had been a strange animal there and that he had had to play his drum to keep the animal dancing. The father listened and told the story to the aunt, who scoffed at the boy.

'There are no strange animals at that place,' she said. 'You must be making all this up.'

But the father believed the boy and said that the next day they would all go to the fruit place with him. The aunt thought that this was a waste of time, but she was not going to miss any chance of shouting, and so she came too.

When the family reached the tree there was no strange animal. The aunt began to pick fruit from the tree and stuff it into her mouth. Calling to the boy to give her his drum, she hung it on the branch of a tree in a place where he would not be able to get at it easily.

'You must pick fruit,' she shouted to the boy. 'You must not play a drum in idleness.'

The boy obeyed his aunt, but all the time he was listening for any sounds to come from the bush. He knew that sooner or later the strange animal would appear and that they would then all be in danger.

When the strange animal did come, it went

straight to the boy's father and mother and quickly ate them up. Then the aunt tried to run away, but the strange animal ran after her and ate her too. While this was happening, the boy had the time to reach up for his drum from the branch of the fruit tree. Quickly he began to play this drum, which made the strange animal stop looking for people to eat and begin to dance.

As the boy played his drum faster and faster, the strange animal danced more and more quickly. Eventually the boy played so fast that the animal had to spit out the father and the mother. The boy was very pleased with this and began to play more slowly. At this, the strange animal's dancing became slower.

'You must play your drum fast again,' the boy's father said. 'Then the strange animal will have to spit out your aunt.'

'Do I have to?' the boy asked, disappointed that he would not be allowed to leave the aunt in the stomach of the strange animal.

'Yes,' the boy's father said sternly. 'You must.'

Reluctantly, the boy again began to play the drum and the strange animal began to dance more quickly. After a few minutes it was dancing so quickly that it had to spit out the aunt. Then darkness came and the strange animal went back to its cave.

The aunt was very quiet during the journey

back home. The next day she was quiet as well, and she never shouted at the boy again. Being swallowed by a strange animal had taught the aunt not to waste her time shouting; now, all that she wanted to do was to sit quietly in the sun.

The boy was very happy.

Bad Uncles

The Chief Kgalabetla was known by all to be a good chief. He was not one to take sides with one person against another, but would find the things on which they could all agree and chose those as the things to do. Nor would he allocate good land to one man every year and bad land to another; rather, he would share these good things amongst all the people who lived over in that place.

This chief was also very old. He had seen more things than anybody else in the village and he could remember the details of everything that had happened. He could also remember cattle, and could tell which beasts came from which place, and who their parents were. This was a very great talent, and people who heard him talking about cattle would stand there with their mouths open in wonderment. They all said that it was remarkable good fortune to have such a wise chief in their midst.

But unfortunately, Chief Kgalabetla was extremely old. He was the oldest man in the village by far, although there were two women who were older than he was. The chief was always very kind and respectful towards these old women, as they knew a great deal too and they had seen many things happen during their lives.

When the chief called a kgotla meeting the people were very surprised. They were surprised because he had not told them the reason for the meeting beforehand, so when people arrived they were not sure what it would all be about. Some people thought that the meeting had been called to discuss when the rains might be expected to arrive, but others said that this was unlikely. So nobody really knew why the meeting was to be held.

When everybody was assembled at the kgotla, there was much excitement in the crowd. People sat on the ground or stood near the walls and talked to one another in raised voices, wondering what the chief would say. When he arrived, the women made their special calling sound to welcome the wise old man and to show how much his people loved him.

The chief began to speak to the people in his ancient, wavering voice.

'I am very old now,' he said, 'and my ancestors are now calling me. I can hear their voices. They are saying that it is time for me to go.'

At this, the people of the village let out a gasp; the sound was great, like the sound of a storm passing across the sky. Then some of the people began to wail and there were those whose faces were covered with tears. So great was the love of the people for this wise chief that they could not control their sorrow.

'Do not weep for me,' said the chief. 'I have lived for many years and I have done many things. Now it is time to die, because that is what we all must do. But I wish to die a happy man, knowing that you will be in the hands of a good man. My son, Ditshabe, is a good man. I have taught him much of what I know and he can learn the rest himself. You will be well looked after under his care.'

The people knew that this was true. Ditshabe was just like his father, and they had all watched with relief as he grew up, as they knew that they would be safe with a young chief like that. Now that the chief had said this, the people made an effort to be cheerful, and they listened carefully as the chief ordered the preparation of the ceremony and celebrations for Ditshabe's installation.

Ditshabe and his uncles were ordered to go to the cattle post and choose thirty head of cattle to bring back for the celebrations. They were not to stay out at the post, but they were to come back as soon as they could, driving the cattle ahead of them. In the meantime the rest of the young men and women were to practise their songs and get their best clothes ready for the occasion. Everybody had something to do.

It was a long way to the cattle post, and Ditshabe and the uncles were very tired when they arrived. They lost no time, though, in gathering thirty of the best cattle and starting the journey back home.

As they walked, some of the uncles talked amongst themselves and decided that it would be best to kill Ditshabe, so that one of them could be the new chief and could rule the people as he wished. That uncle would look after the other uncles, and they would all be happier than if their nephew were to be the new chief. Halfway through the journey back, the uncles fell upon Ditshabe and struck him with some rocks that they had picked up in the bush. The young man was not expecting this attack. He fell to the ground, his bright blood gushing out on to the dry earth, like a small, red river. The uncles dug a hole and buried him, in a place where there were thorn trees. There was nobody to cry for him; only the sky and the clouds and the trees were the witnesses of this sad event.

As they continued with their journey home, the uncles planned what they would tell the chief and his people when they returned. They would say that Ditshabe had walked off the path to look for something to eat and had not come back. They would say that they had heard a roaring sound, like the sound of a hungry lion, and that he must have been eaten up by this lion, as can sometimes happen.

Shortly after they had planned this story, a brightly coloured bird landed on a tree in front of them. At first they did not see it, but when it began to sing they saw where it was sitting on a branch, beside the thorns.

'Tswiidiii phara tswiidiii phara,' sang the bird. 'Can you kill him just like that? I am going to tell that you have killed Chief Ditshabe.'

The uncles laughed at this bird and told it to go away. Then they continued their journey and were soon back at the village, where they broke the sad news of Ditshabe's having been eaten. There was much crying in the village, and people thought it sad that at the end of such a good life the chief should be greeted with such news about his fine son.

One old woman was very sad. She sat under a tree throughout the following day, thinking about this sad event, when she suddenly heard a bird in the branches above her. She looked up and saw a brightly coloured bird, which sang to her the exact same song that it had sung to the uncles. The old woman listened carefully and went off to tell the chief what the bird had said to her.

The chief was very angry. He ordered a regiment of young men to go to the place that the bird had mentioned. There they found the body of Ditshabe. They carried him back to the chief, tears streaming down their cheeks. Everybody could tell that he had been hit with rocks and not eaten by a lion as the lying uncles had claimed.

The chief called the people together. Even after the death of his son, with the body lying there before him, the body of the boy he had loved so much, he spoke with dignity and firmness. The uncles all started to point fingers at one another, this one blaming that one, and that one blaming this one. The chief silenced them, and asked the people what should be done with the uncles.

The people said that the uncles should be killed. And so this happened.

Why Elephant And Hyena Live Far From People

An inquisitive boy once asked his grandmother why elephants and hyenas lived so far away from people. He thought that this might be because the elephant was so large, and needed great empty places in which to roam. As for the hyena, the boy thought that he might live far away from people because he was an animal who liked to wander at night and needed quiet paths for his wandering.

The grandmother listened to what the boy said and shook her head. She knew the answer to his questions, which she had been told many years before. Now she told the boy.

*   *   *

There was a great chief once. He had many fields and there were lots of people who lived on his lands. After the rains had come and made the ground wet, the people would prepare their oxen for ploughing. Then they would cut into the soft ground and the children would put in lines of seeds. More rains would come and the seeds would grow

101

into tall plants with heavy ears of corn.

There were people who lived near a river in that chief's lands. They planted their fields carefully and all about their new plants they built fences made out of sticks and pieces of thorn tree. No cow would dare to wander into these fields and eat the plants, as the thorns at the edge would tear into her skin. For this reason the plants grew tall and the people would all think of the delicious corn that would soon be cooking in their pots.

One morning one of the boys who looked after the plants saw that a great hole had been torn through the fence of thorns. He ran into the field and cried out as he saw the damage that had been done to the plants—where there had been rows of corn there was now only flattened stalks and scattered leaves.

This boy's father wept when he saw what had happened.

'Now we shall have no food,' he said, picking up the broken stalk of the tallest plant. 'We shall be hungry this year.'

That afternoon they rebuilt the fence, hoping that it would stop the creature from visiting their fields that night. The next morning, though, the creature had been again, making a large hole in the fence of thorns and eating up more plants than before. Everybody in the village wept that day.

In another part of that chief's lands there were other people who also felt sad. They had a great field of pumpkins, also protected by a fence of thorns. By night some creature of great cunning had burrowed underneath the fence and eaten many pumpkins. There were still some pumpkins left, but they knew that if the creature visited them again then all their pumpkins would be gone. For those people, who ate only pumpkins, this was a terrible thing to happen.

When they heard of the misfortune of the people who lived by the river, the pumpkin people walked across to the houses by the river and held a meeting.

'We have lost almost all our corn,' said the river people. 'A great creature pushed through our fence of thorns as if it were nothing.'

The pumpkin people nodded and said: 'That creature must be an elephant. Only an elephant could do that.'

Then they told the river people what had happened to their field of pumpkins and the river people nodded their heads and said: 'That must be a hyena. Only a hyena would have the cunning to dig his way under a fence of thorns.'

*   *   *

There were some animals who heard the people talking in this way. They heard the sad voices of the men and saw the place where the tears had fallen on the ground. These animals, who had kind hearts, were saddened and they went off into the bush and told the other animals about what had happened. Even some birds heard the story and began to sing sad songs about it.

Of course it was not long before the elephant and the hyena heard what was being said about them. All the other animals now said that they were wicked and that they should not have caused so much sadness to the growers of the crops. The elephant felt ashamed when he realized what the other animals were saying about him and so he went to see the hyena.

'Everybody is calling us evil,' he said. 'They shake their heads when they mention our names and say that there is enough food for everybody without our stealing the food of other people.'

The hyena felt ashamed too and he lowered his head to the ground and howled through his yellow teeth.

'I do not like to think of my name being so bad,' he said to the elephant. 'Let's go to the chief and ask him to change our names.'

The elephant thought that this was a good idea. Once he was no longer called an elephant, then he would be able to hold his head up again among the other animals.

'We shall set off early tomorrow morning,' he said to the hyena. 'It is a long way to that chief's house and we shall need all day to travel.'

*   *   *

The next morning the two friends set off just as the first light of the sun came over the top of the hills. They walked through the bush all morning and stopped only for a short time at midday. Throughout the afternoon they walked, following the path that led to the chief's village, watching the sun go slowly down the sky. At last, just as the sun sank and the first of the stars began to glimmer above them, they saw the fires of the chief's village.

The chief's messenger welcomed them at the entrance to the village. He had heard of the bad name of the elephant and the hyena, but because they were visitors to the chief he did not show his feelings about them.

'We have come to have our names changed,' explained the hyena, his red eyes glowing in the darkness.

The chief's messenger listened politely and then said: 'I'm sorry, but it's too late for the chief to change your names. He can do that tomorrow morning when it is light and he can see what he is doing. I shall get some boys to show you to your sleeping quarters for the night.'

A tall boy came and took the elephant to the place where he was to sleep. Because he was so large, this had to be in a field. The boy wished the elephant a good night and then he took the hyena to his place. Not being so large, the hyena was able to sleep in a hut, and was given the skin of a water-buck with which to cover himself.

'At night there are only stars in the sky,' said the boy. 'You will need this skin to keep you warm.'

The hyena thanked him and settled down in a corner of the hut and began to cover himself with the skin. The boy closed the door of the hut and went back to the chief's messenger.

'Our guests have gone to bed,' he said.

'Good,' said the messenger. 'They can speak to the chief when the sun comes up and he can change their names then. That will make them happy.'

*   *   *

Just before the first light of the morning, the hyena crept out of his hut and made his way to the elephant's sleeping field. He walked low down, his head dropped, as if he were sneaking away in shame—just the way that all hyenas walk. Standing in the field, waiting for his friend, the elephant also had his head lowered, his tusks almost touching the ground.

'I am very ashamed of myself,' the elephant said, even before the hyena could wish him good morning. 'They put me in this field of corn to sleep and during the night I ate it all.'

The hyena looked at the field. It was covered with the stalks of felled plants, as if a great wind had blown upon it during the night.

'I am also ashamed,' he said to the elephant. 'They gave me a skin last night to cover myself and I ate it all up. Only the end of the tail is left.'

The two bad friends were now too ashamed to go before the chief to ask him to change their names. Instead they ran into the bush and found places far from people where they could live. They were still called elephant and hyena and all the other animals still said bad things about these names. That is why the elephant and the hyena live far away.

The Wife Who Could Not Work

When Kumalo saw the beautiful girl at her father's house he knew that he would have to marry her. The girl was shy and did not look at him, but he could tell that she was beyond doubt the most beautiful girl in that part of the country.

'How many cattle would I have to give you to marry your daughter?' he asked the father.

The father looked at Kumalo and could tell that he was a rich man.

'That girl is very beautiful,' he said.

'I can see that,' said Kumalo. 'You must be proud of her.'

'The man who marries her will have to give me lots of cattle,' went on the father.

'How many?' asked Kumalo. 'I am sure that I will have that many.'

'Fifty,' said the father.

Even for Kumalo that was a very large number of cattle, but he agreed with the father that he would give them to him in return for the privilege of marrying his daughter. The father seemed pleased and called other people across to witness the bargain.

'I must warn you about something,' he said

109

after they had agreed on the day when the cattle would be delivered. 'Many beautiful girls cannot work very hard. That girl is so beautiful that she cannot work at all.'

Kumalo was surprised by this, but quickly promised that the girl would never have to do any work in his household.

'That is good,' said the father. 'She will be happy with you.'

*　　*　　*

There were other women who lived at Kumalo's place. These were aunts and cousins and other relatives, and they all had large huts where they kept all their property and ate their meals at night. They were happy living with Kumalo and they were pleased when he told them that he would be getting married. They prepared a great feast for his new wife and when she arrived they all cried with joy when they saw how beautiful she was. On the first day that she spent at Kumalo's house, people came from all the nearby hills to look at the beautiful girl. Then they went back and told their families about her beauty and about how many cattle Kumalo had given her father.

Kumalo explained to everybody at his house that his new wife was too delicate to do any work.

'This beautiful girl will have to sit in the

110

shade all day,' he said. 'She can watch you work, but she must do nothing herself. I have promised her father that.'

So, while the other women performed the many tasks that had to be carried out around a house, the new wife sat in the doorway of one of the huts and watched them go about their tasks. She said nothing while she watched, but the women could feel her eyes on them as they worked.

After a few weeks, Kumalo's senior cousin complained to one of the other women about the new wife.

'She sits there all day,' she said bitterly. 'She eats her share of the food—and more—but she does nothing in return.'

The other woman agreed.

'I have seen her too,' she said. 'There is no reason why she should not do some work as well. She has the strength.'

Other women, hearing these remarks, joined in the protests. They did not say anything to Kumalo himself, knowing that he had promised his father-in-law that the new wife should not work, but every day now they stared at the new wife and tried to make her feel guilty about not working. The new wife, however, just stared back at the other women, a sweet smile on her face.

Eventually the senior cousin decided that she would act. She had had enough of watching the new wife do nothing while the rest of them laboured and she went up to her and told her that the time had come for her to work. Kumalo had gone to a far place to buy cattle and would not be back until the next day—it would be safe for them to make the new wife work.

The new wife did not object. Rising to her feet, she asked the senior cousin what she had to do and quietly took the calabash that was given to her.

'It is easy work just to fill this small calabash with water,' said the cousin. 'Even a beautiful woman like you can do that.'

The other women stopped their work and watched the new wife walk off towards the river. As she disappeared into the thick grass that grew there, they all laughed.

'At long last that lazy woman is having to work,' they said. 'Today at least she cannot sit in her doorway and watch us working.'

*   *   *

The new wife found the place in the river where water was to be drawn. She filled the calabash with ease and then turned round to begin her walk back. As she walked across the sandbank at the edge of the river, though, she felt the weight of the calabash getting greater and greater. She sensed the sand coming up around her ankles and found that it was more and more difficult to lift her feet. Then she found that her feet were sinking and that no matter what she did she could not free them. She was so light and delicate that the weight of the calabash was pushing her down into the ground, and in the time that it takes a bird to fly from one tree to another she had sunk completely out of sight.

The other women waited for her to return to the house so that they could laugh at her and send her back to the river for more water. After they had waited for some time, they began to feel uneasy.

'Perhaps she has run away,' said one of the women.

'She would not do that,' another said. 'She must be hiding. She is trying to give us a fright.'

The senior cousin decided that they should go and find the new wife and so the women all left their work and followed the footprints down to the river bank. They searched and searched all along the river and in the bush beside it, but there was no trace of the new wife. Wailing loudly, they returned to the house wondering what they would be able to tell Kumalo when he came back the following day.

'We shall say that she was eaten by a lion,' suggested one of the women. 'That way he will not be able to blame us.'

*   *   *

Kumalo came back to the house early the next morning bringing with him the cattle that he had bought. He was in a good mood after having bought fine cattle, but his smile faded when he saw that his new wife was not in her usual place.

'Where is my beautiful wife?' he asked the women. 'She was sitting in her doorway when I left.'

The women all looked at the senior cousin, who answered with the lie that she had prepared.

'A lion ate her,' she said. 'We tried to stop it, but it was too hungry.'

Kumalo looked at his senior cousin.

'You are lying,' he said. 'A lion would not choose a delicate girl like that. It would rather eat a fat woman like you.'

The cousin said nothing, but when Kumalo shook his fist at her she told the truth.

'We only asked her to do a little work,' she whined. 'It was not too hard.'

Kumalo did not listen any more. Immediately he ran to a man who lived nearby who knew all about finding people who had been lost. This man listened to Kumalo's sad story and then told him what to do.

'Go to the side of the river,' he said. 'Beat this small drum and get a fat woman to jump hard on the ground. That will bring back your beautiful wife.'

Kumalo ran back to his house, the sound of his beating heart loud in his ears. He called the senior cousin to follow him and made his way quickly to the side of the river. There he played the drum, while the senior cousin jumped up and down on the sand. It was hard for her to do this, as she was so fat, but each time she showed signs of slowing down Kumalo would shout at her and urge her on.

At last they saw the sand parting and the head of the new wife slowly appeared.

'Jump faster!' ordered Kumalo, and as the senior cousin continued to jump the rest of the new wife was forced up out of the sand.

When the new wife had risen completely out of the sand, Kumalo went forward and embraced her tenderly. Then he led her back to the place where she used to sit and watch the women working. The senior cousin, ashamed of what they had done, promised they would never ask the new wife to work again. Although he was angry with the other women, Kumalo forgave them, and that night they all had a feast to celebrate the return of the new wife to her husband.

Bad Blood

There was a woman who lived in a village near the end of the land. This woman had two sons, one called Diepe and the other Diepetsana. They were very poor people and they did not have a great deal to eat. Their granary was never more than half full and they wore very shabby clothes. Sometimes they had no clothes at all, and had to wear old rags and leaves to preserve their modesty. It was not easy being that poor.

In the same village there was a young man called Dimo. He was not as poor as these other two, as he had married the daughter of a rich man. He had everything that he needed in this life, including a great deal of food. This food, which was rich and good, had made him quite fat.

This Dimo asked Diepe whether he could come and help him at the cattle post of his wife's parents. There was much to be done there, he said, and they would be looked after well. Because he was poor and had nothing else to do, Diepe agreed to accompany Dimo to this place, which was very far away, and on the edge of the place where nobody lived but

117

only wild animals.

During their first evening at the cattle post, Dimo's wife brought water to the hut to wash the hands of the men before they had food. Dimo asked Diepe whose food he would be eating and said that because it belonged to the parents of his wife, it was not right that Diepe should eat it. So Diepe went to bed without any food and his stomach was empty and painful within him.

That night, Dimo went outside and killed some sheep which were in a stockade. Then he took the blood of the sheep and put it in a calabash. Back in the hut, while Diepe was fast asleep, Dimo put the sheep blood all over the sleeping man's face. The next morning, when the parents of Dimo's wife went out to look at their animals they found that the sheep had all been killed.

'Who has done this wicked thing?' they asked.

Dimo pointed at Diepe, and said, 'His face is covered with sheep blood. Look! That is the person who has done this wicked thing.'

The parents then said that Diepe should be killed for having done this, and that happened that afternoon. Dimo was pleased, and when he went back to the place where Diepe's brother lived, he told Diepe's mother that her son was being well looked after in that other place and that now he had come to take

Diepetsana to join him. Diepetsana was very pleased to go with Dimo, although he could tell that there was something wrong. Diepetsana was a traditional doctor and would be very good at intuiting such things when he was older. But even now he could tell that there was something wicked planned, and he took with him two very important fly whisks that were good for all sorts of tasks.

They reached the cattle post and Diepetsana saw that there was no sign of his brother. That night he slept in a hut, but before he lay down he set up the fly whisks so that they would see if anybody came in at night. One was placed at the foot of his sleeping mat and another at the top.

In the depths of the night the fly whisk at the top of the sleeping mat sang out: 'Who is this entering?'

And the reply came from the fly whisk at the bottom of the sleeping mat: 'Isn't it Dimo?'

'What does he have on his hand?' sang the top fly whisk.

And the bottom fly whisk sang 'Isn't it blood?'

Dimo was very frightened when this happened and he withdrew from the hut. A few minutes later he plucked up the courage to enter, and the same thing happened. And so it went on until the morning, when the parents of Dimo's wife awoke to find their son-in-law outside the hut with a large gourd of sheep's blood and the sheep all dead upon the ground.

They were very angry and killed Dimo on the spot. They were pleased with Diepetsana, though, and they rewarded him handsomely. He was now a rich man and he looked after his mother well, so that she was no longer poor. Their life had changed, although they still felt sad for the loss of Diepe and thought often of their brother and son who had now gone.

The Sad Story Of Tortoise And Snail

Tortoise and snail had been boys together and loved each other with a deep love. When either was away, the other was unable to sleep, but would lie awake, wondering when his friend would return.

Although as boys they had done everything together, their work as adults had been different. Tortoise had become a farmer, and had done nothing but grow crops; Snail, by contrast, had become a trader, and had many trading posts in all parts of the country.

Although Snail was happy in his work as a trader, and was always able to buy all the food that he needed, he longed to do what Tortoise did. When he saw Tortoise surveying his fields of ripening crops, he thought of the pleasure that must come from growing such fine food. There was no such pleasure in trading, where the only satisfaction was in making more and more money. Snail knew that this was not a satisfaction that would last forever, and so he went to Tortoise and spoke to him about his dream of becoming a farmer.

'If you give me some grain,' he said to his friend, 'then I shall be able to plant it in a small field that I have.'

Tortoise was suspicious of Snail's request. He wondered why Snail wished to grow grain when he was rich enough to buy all the grain he could ever need. Could it be that Snail was trying to prove that he was cleverer than he? If that was so, it was a bad way to treat a friend and was not a request that he would be prepared to meet.

'I shall give you some corn to plant,' he said to Snail. 'Come back tomorrow and it will be ready for you.'

Snail left Tortoise's house, happy that his plan to be a farmer seemed to be going so well. What he did not know, though, was that the moment he had left, Tortoise had taken a handful of corn and had put it into boiling water. There he left it until it was thoroughly boiled. Tortoise knew that in this state it would never germinate and Snail's field would grow nothing but weeds.

Snail planted his seeds when the first rains arrived. There were good rains that year, and in Tortoise's fields the crops grew tall and strong. Other people, too, had good crops, except for Snail, who spent his time cutting back weeds and examining the ground to see when the corn would grow. Tortoise said nothing about the failure of Snail's crop, although in private he was laughing. When Snail told him that next year he would try a new piece of land, Tortoise just nodded.

'I shall give you some good seeds,' he said. 'They will surely grow next year.'

Snail planted the new seeds given to him by Tortoise. The rains were heavy again that year and there was much growth throughout the country, but in Snail's fields only weeds grew. Tortoise was sympathetic and made suggestions about how Snail might improve his farming. Snail, however, was now suspicious of the seed he had been given and when, the following year, Tortoise again gave him corn seed, he took it to hare. Hare looked at the seed and shook his head.

'This seed has been boiled,' he pronounced. 'It is good only for eating—here, try it.'

Snail took one of the corn seeds and put it in his mouth. The seed had all the softness of boiled corn and the taste of his friend's deception was bitter in his mouth. Snail decided that he must have his revenge on Tortoise. Going to see his mother, he asked her if she could pretend to be dead. Then he went to Tortoise and told him of his misfortune, asking him to help him to bury his mother. Tortoise was quick to console him, and told him how sad it must be to lose a mother.

Snails bury their mothers in special places, and it was to one of these places that they carried what Tortoise thought was the body of

Snail's mother. In fact, the body was nothing but a banana stem wrapped up in leaves, and the tears that Snail wept were not real tears.

Later, Snail asked Tortoise to come and pray with him at the grave, which was in front of a small bush. The two animals said their prayers and then, to Tortoise's surprise, they saw money falling in front of them.

'It is from my mother,' Snail said. 'If you pray at the grave of your mother, the mother will give you money.'

Tortoise believed this. He had not seen Snail's mother hiding in the bush, and he had not heard her chuckles as she threw the money out before them. Snail's words remained in his mind for the rest of the day, and by evening he had made his plan.

The next morning Tortoise arrived at his mother's house, looking very sad.

'Why are you so sad?' his mother asked. 'Has something terrible happened to you?'

Tortoise shook his head. Then he looked at his mother and spoke angrily.

'Why are you still alive?' he asked. 'Do you expect me to die before you?'

Tortoise's mother was surprised by this, but she answered calmly.

'I do not think I should die yet,' she said. 'There is no need.'

Tortoise became angrier. 'But are you not older than Snail's mother, who has already died?' he shouted. 'Do you expect to live forever?'

'Not forever,' Tortoise's mother answered. 'I want to live only until I have eaten all the food I was meant to eat.'

When he heard this answer, Tortoise stormed off. A few hours later he was back, carrying with him twenty baskets of food and twenty buckets of water. He put this burden down in front of his mother and told her to eat and drink, as this was about as much food and water as she was due by nature to consume.

'But I'm not hungry,' his mother said. 'So you must go away, and take the food elsewhere.'

This reply drove Tortoise into a rage. He lifted up a stick that was lying nearby and he brought this down heavily on his mother's head. She died.

Snail helped him carry the body of his mother to her grave. Then, standing before the grave, Tortoise began to pray. No money came. Tortoise looked at Snail. Snail laughed.

An Old Man Who Saved Some Ungrateful People

In a certain village there lived people who were both happy and rich. They had very good fields there, and each year they harvested so much grain that their grain bins were full to overflowing. Some of the grain bins were so full, in fact, that the tree trunks which served as their legs broke and tipped the bins to the ground. This did not matter, as there was far more grain than was needed.

The birds heard about this village and decided that it would be a good place for birds to live. They arrived one morning, in a great fluttering cloud, and settled themselves on trees around the fields. Then, when the people had finished their work in the fields, the birds flew down and ate as much grain as they could manage. Then they flew back to their places in the trees and slept until the next morning.

The people were worried when they saw the next morning how much of the grain had been eaten by these greedy birds. They shouted at the trees and shook their fists, but the birds just sang and paid no attention to the people below them.

The people returned to the village and got out all their bows and arrows. Then they walked back to the fields and aimed the arrows at the birds.

It was easy for the birds to avoid the arrows. As they saw them coming through the air, they just flew up until the arrows had passed. Then they landed on their branches again and began to sing.

'We shall soon starve,' the women said to the headman. 'If you do nothing, all the people in this village will stop being fat and will become very thin.'

The headman knew that what they said was right. And yet he could think of no way in which they could deal with the birds. If their arrows did not work, then there was no other weapon at their disposal.

They talked and talked about the problem until one of the young men said:

'There is always that old man—the one we all chased away from the village. He knows many magic things and may be able to do something about the birds.'

Everybody was silent. They had all been thinking the same thing but nobody had been courageous enough to talk about it. The old man had been chased away because of his spells and now they were going to have to beg him to come back again.

'Where does he live now?' asked the

headman. 'I think we shall have to go and speak to him.'

The young man explained that he had seen the old man living in a bush not far away. He would be able to take the headman there and show him the place.

*   *   *

When the headman arrived at the bush in which the old man lived, he was saddened to see him in such a state. All his clothes were now rags and his cheeks were hollow. There were few leaves left on the bush, as the old man had been forced to eat leaves to deal with the great hunger which plagued him.

The headman greeted the old man and said how sorry he was that he had not seen him for such a long time. The old man looked at him, but said nothing.

'We are having a problem with birds,' the head man then said. 'Although we have good crops, the birds come down from the trees and eat all our grain. Soon we will be as poor as you are.'

'You should shoot the birds,' the old man said. 'That's how you solve that problem.'

'These birds are too clever,' the headman said. 'When our arrows come close to them, they hop up in the air and are unharmed.'

The old man thought for a moment before

he spoke again.

'I cannot help you,' he said. 'You made me leave that place before, and now I'm living in this new place.'

The headman had feared that the old man would say something like this. He begged him to think again, and when the old man still said no, he begged him again. At last the old man agreed to come, although he was unhappy to leave the bush in which he was living.

Before they returned to the village, the old man went to a number of secret places which he knew and collected roots and other substances that he would need for his work. Then they went back to the village, where all the people were waiting to welcome the old man back into their midst.

*　　　*　　　*

The next morning, the old man called everybody in the village to the door of his hut. From a pouch which he had with him, he took out powders which he had made from the roots and other substances. Everybody was then told to dip the tips of their arrows into this powder and, when they had done this, to go down to the fields and wait for him to come.

The birds watched the people gathering at the edge of the fields and laughed among themselves. The leader of the birds fluffed up his feathers and began to sing a special bird song which was all about how birds enjoyed eating the food of foolish people. Just as he sang, the old man took an arrow from a young man's bow and shot it toward the singing bird. The bird rose into the air, laughing at the useless weapons of the people below, but the arrow followed him upwards and pierced the centre of his heart.

All the other birds were silent when they saw what had happened to their leader. Before they could rise from their branches, though, many other arrows came up through the air and struck them down. After a few minutes, there were very few birds left, and these few took wing for the hills.

*   *   *

The village people were so happy at the fact that they had been saved that they took the old man to the largest hut they had and made him their new chief. They gave him four cows and a great supply of beer. Whenever he needed anything, he had only to ask, and it would be delivered to him.

The old man was happy to be a chief, and he ruled well. He never made unfair decisions, and he never took more than his fair share of anything. When people were squabbling over

131

some little matter, he would settle the argument wisely. Everybody was content at the way he ruled.

After a while, some people began to talk about how the old man must still have powers to work magic.

'If he did it before,' they said, 'then he might do it again. He knows how these powders work.'

Other people agreed.

'Perhaps one day he might use his magic against us,' one man said. 'If he did that, we would be powerless to stop him.'

'We would be like the birds,' another said. 'He could shoot an arrow into our heart.'

Such talk was soon going all around the village. Eventually, when enough people had heard it, they gathered in a crowd outside the old man's hut and shouted out for him to leave. The old man looked out of his door and was surprised to see the people standing there.

'I have done no wrong,' he said. 'Why are you asking me to leave?'

'Because you are too clever,' the people said. 'We are frightened of you.'

The old man went back into his hut but soon came out again. Carrying the pouch with his powders in it, he left the village and returned to the bush where he had been living before he became chief. Satisfied with their work, the people had a party the next day to celebrate the departure of the old man. They did not see the birds sitting on the branches, watching the party.

*   *   *

When the people saw that the birds had returned, they began to wail.

'We shall have to find the old man again,' they said. 'We must bring him back to the village or we shall again lose all our crops.'

As the birds descended on the fields and began to eat the grain, four of the most important men from the village ran off to find the old man. It took them some time to find him, but at last they reached the bush where he lived.

'You must come back to the village,' they said. 'We shall give you back your hut and your cows. You must come back.'

The old man looked at the ungrateful people who stood before him. Then he looked at the bush, with its few leaves and the hard ground around it.

'No,' he said.

Lazy Baboons

It is well known that a long time ago people and animals lived together in a contented way. In those days, animals could talk, although they later lost the ability to do this. Nobody knows why this happened, but from that day onwards people and animals just had to look at one another and guess what the other was thinking.

It is equally well known that in those days the baboons were very lazy. They lived together with people under a chief, although the baboons preferred the rocky places. The people and the baboons would work together, all of them helping plough the fields and harvest the crops. Some of the crops would go to people, and some would go to the baboons. It all worked very well.

Once, after the rains had started, the chief announced that it was time to start ploughing. The people all went off, together with the baboons, to plough the largest of the fields, which was the chief's field. This was a very difficult task, and it took a long time. The people worked hard, but the baboons did not. They were content to eat the results of all this hard labour, but they were unwilling to do their full share of the work. They had a song which they sang, and its words were:

Rititse rititse, we are afraid of ploughing,
Rititse rititse, we are afraid of ploughing.

That is how the baboons behaved, and the people saw it and talked amongst themselves of the laziness of baboons. They still talk of this today, even when the baboons have lost the ability to sing and the tune of this song has been forgotten.

Great Snake

When the chief called Mikizi died there was much discussion as to who should be the next chief. Mikizi had a son, but the mother of that boy did not want her son to be chief.

'He will never have any peace if he is a chief,' she said. 'Every day there will be people asking him to do things. This is a boy who likes to sleep. If he becomes a chief, he will never be able to sit on his stool and sleep all day.'

The elders all knew that there was no point in trying to make that boy a chief and so they called all the witchdoctors in those parts to come to a meeting to help in the finding of a new chief. The leader of these witchdoctors said that there was only one way to find a new chief and that this was the way they should use.

'There is a hill near here,' he said. 'In the rocks around that hill there is a very large snake. Whoever can capture that great snake and bring it back here shall be made into the new chief.'

The elders agreed that this was a very good way of choosing a new chief, although they doubted if anybody would be brave enough to try to capture that great snake. When a short boy came forward and said that he wished to try, they all laughed.

'Don't be so stupid,' they said to him. 'Short boys can never catch such large snakes.'

'I should like to try,' insisted the boy.

The elders said that he could not try but the boy kept asking again and again for their permission. At last they had had enough of his pestering and told him that he would be allowed to try.

'The snake will kill you,' they warned him. 'As you go down its throat, you should remember these words of ours.'

*　　　*　　　*

The short boy set off towards the hill where the great snake lived. As he left the village, he heard people crying, and he knew that these were his friends who thought that he would never return. He paid no attention to their sorrow, though, as he knew that he would be able to capture the snake and bring it back to the village.

When he reached the first rocks that lay littered about the bottom of the hill, he stopped and listened to the sounds which were carried on the wind. He heard the swishing of the dry grass and the movement of the leaves in the trees. He heard the faint trickle of water and the sound of an eagle hunting high above

138

the ground. And then he heard something else—the sound of a snake hissing.

The boy walked on until he was standing at the bottom of the hill. The sound he had heard was now quite loud and before much time had passed he saw the head of the great snake appear from a crack in the rocks. The snake looked angry that a short boy should have come to disturb him and with a sudden sliding it shot out and darted towards the boy's feet.

When he saw the snake coming towards him, the boy turned round and began to run away from the hill. He ran as fast as he could, but the snake just laughed at those short legs and drew closer and closer to the fleeing boy.

Looking over his shoulder, the short boy saw where the snake was and heard its laughter. He continued to run, but as he did so he took from his shoulder a calabash that he had hung there and began to drop things from it. First he dropped a lizard and then he dropped some frogs. After that he dropped some other small insects.

The snake came to the lizard and stopped. For a moment it seemed uncertain whether to carry on after the short boy, but then it opened its great mouth and swallowed the lizard. After it had done this, it resumed its chase of the boy, only to stop again when it came to the frogs jumping about on the ground.

The snake gobbled up the frogs, although it

took it some time to catch them all. Then, its belly heavy with food, it slid on after the boy, only to stop again when it came to the insects.

By the time that the snake had eaten all the things that the boy dropped from the calabash, they were just outside the village fence. The boy called out to the elders that he was back and walked slowly through the gap in the fence.

'So,' called out one of the elders. 'You are back. Where is the great snake?'

The boy said nothing at first, then, with all the eyes of the village upon him, he turned round and pointed to the gate. As he did so, the great snake, fat and slow from all its eating, slid heavily into the village.

The people let out a great sigh when they saw the snake arrive and immediately the young men pinned it to the ground with sticks. The short boy stood before the elders and asked them if he could now be made the chief. The elders were surprised that such a short boy could be so brave but they remembered their promise and agreed to make him chief.

Later, when he was chief, the short boy grew taller.

The Girl Who Married A Lion

Nearly everybody was happy when Kumalo's daughter married. Kumalo was pleased with the many fine cattle which his new son-in-law had given him; his wife was happy that she would no longer have to worry about what sort of man her daughter would marry; and the daughter herself was pleased that she had found such a fine, strong husband.

Only the new wife's brother was unhappy.

'I think that my sister has married a lion,' he said to his friends. 'This is really a lion disguised as a man.'

Nobody took this seriously and they laughed at the young man when he said such things. But the brother knew that what he said was true, and he could not bring himself to talk to this new brother-in-law of his.

'I cannot talk to a lion,' he said.

Several years passed and the wife had two strong sons, who were as handsome as their father. Still the wife's brother muttered that the husband was a lion disguised as a man and still he refused to do anything with his brother-in-law.

'You're being stupid,' Kumalo said. 'Look at

141

all the cattle that my daughter's husband gave me when he married her. Where would a lion get such cattle?'

The young man could not think of an answer to that question, but he refused to change his mind. He knew that sooner or later there would be trouble. And indeed one day his sister came to him and asked to talk to him in private.

'I am worried about this husband of mine,' she whispered to her brother. 'He has a strange smell on him.'

'What sort of smell?' the brother asked.

The woman shrugged her shoulders. 'It is a very strange smell,' she said. 'I cannot describe it.'

In order to help his sister, the young man agreed to go to her hut and to smell some of the things that belonged to the husband. The husband was out at the time, and so it was easy for the wife to show the things that he carried with him. The brother smelled them and frowned.

'That is lion smell,' he said.

The woman was very worried and she went with her brother to speak to their father. The old man was not happy to hear this news. He did not want to believe that his son-in-law was a lion, and so he said that they would test him to see if he really was a lion.

'We will put a goat outside his hut at night,'

he said. 'If the goat is gone in the morning, then we will know that a lion has eaten it. That will prove that he is a lion.'

Everyone agreed that this would be a good test and that night a goat was tethered outside the son-in-law's hut. The next morning, the father and the son went to the hut and saw that only the bones of the goat were left.

'No man would eat a goat like that,' the son said triumphantly. 'He is surely a lion.'

The old man had to agree. It was hard to admit that such a thing had happened, but he had no other choice. There was only one thing to do: to fetch their spears and to chase the son-in-law away from the home. The son-in-law was angry, of course, and tried to resist, but he could not fight the sharp points of the spears. As he ran off into the bush, both the father and his son saw that the marks where his feet had been were marks of a lion. This proved to them that they had been right. The woman was upset to have lost her fine husband, but she understood that it would have been impossible for her to continue to live with a lion. At any time her husband might have threatened to eat her.

Her brother thought that she would now be happy, but she came to see him again and it was clear that once again she was anxious.

'If my husband was a lion,' she said to her brother, 'then what are my two sons?'

The brother thought for a moment. He had not considered this problem and it made him worried. He loved his two nephews and it would be a sad blow if they turned out to be lions when they grew up. He looked closely at the two boys, but there were no signs that they were lions.

'We must be quite sure about this,' he said to his sister. 'We will have to test the boys in a special way.'

Making a cage out of thin trees, the brother carried this to a lonely place where lions liked to walk. He put the cage on the ground and went back to fetch the two boys. Then he took them to the cage and told them to get into it and sit there.

'I am testing this cage,' he explained to the boys. 'I want to see if it is strong enough to give protection against lions. I will come back tonight and see if the lions have managed to break into it.'

The younger boy became very scared of being left in the cage, but the elder one comforted him.

'Our uncle would not put us in danger,' he said. 'This cage must be strong enough to keep the lions away.'

The uncle had told his nephews that he was going back to his hut, but in fact he hid in some trees nearby and waited to see what happened. After a while, two lions walked up to the cage and began to sniff at it. The two boys cowered in the corner of the cage, and the uncle could hear the younger one weeping.

After they had sniffed at the cage, the lions began to roar. Then they started to dash at the cage, shaking the thin wooden bars with their great weight. The two boys seemed very frightened and the uncle decided that if he did not go down to their rescue they would soon be eaten.

Leaping from his tree, the uncle rushed towards the lions, waving a long spear in his hand. The lions saw the spear and ran off into the bush, leaving the two frightened boys in the cage.

'Thank you, Uncle,' the elder boy said. 'I thought that we might be eaten by the lions.'

The uncle smiled as he let his nephews out of the cage. Now he knew that they were not lions, for if they had been lions the real lions would have smelled it and would not have tried to attack them.

'Your sons are not lions,' the uncle said to the boys' mother.

'I am glad,' she said.

Two Bad Friends

When an important chief died down in that far part of the country, there were many people who went to see him buried. It was a time of great sorrow, as this chief had ruled over many people for many years and had been the son of one who had served with a very great chief.

Two friends, who liked to play tricks on one another and on other people, decided that they would go to the burial too. They walked past a place where there were many mourners, all sitting under a tree and singing about how sad they were that the chief had died.

'We are very sad too,' the two friends said. 'We are sad because that great chief was our father.'

When they heard this, the people under the tree were surprised. They asked the two friends if they were sure that the chief was their father, and they replied that they were.

'You must give us money,' one friend said. 'You must give us money because we are the sons of the one who has died.'

The people knew that they should do this, but they were unwilling to give money to people whom they did not know.

'If you come with us to the grave,' they said, 'then we shall be able to find out whether you really are the sons of that great chief.'

The two friends agreed to do this. There was no reason for them to refuse to go to the grave, and already they were thinking of ways of fooling these people under the tree.

When they reached the grave, there were many people milling about, calling out in sorrow and saying how sad they were that the chief had gone. Even those who did not like the chief were there, saying that they were more sorry than any others. If the chief had been alive, he would have been pleased to see so many of his enemies shedding so many tears on his death.

The people from under the tree told one of the friends to stand by the side of the grave. He did this, but while he was moving into that position, the other friend hid in a bush which grew near the edge of the grave.

Then one of the people from under the tree called out into the sky.

'Is it true that these men are your sons?'

Everybody was surprised when a voice called out:

'They are my sons. And you must give them lots of money.'

'The chief himself has spoken to us,' the people from under the tree said. 'We must do as he says.'

The other friend then slipped out of the bush. The voice had been his, of course, but everybody had thought that it had come from the grave.

The two friends stood respectfully by the grave while people walked past and put money into a box which one of the friends had with him. Then, crying loudly to show how sad they were, they walked back to the house of one of them.

'I shall keep the money here until it is counted,' said the friend whose house it was. 'Then one day you may come and claim your half share.'

*   *   *

The next day, the friend returned to the house of the friend who had kept the money. That friend's wife greeted him sadly and told him that his friend was unfortunately very ill and would have to stay in his bed for a long time.

'He will not be able to give you your money,' she said. 'He is too ill to do that.'

'Then I shall wait,' said the other friend. 'I shall wait by his bedside until he is better.'

'That may not be for a few years,' said the wife. 'He says that he is very ill.'

'I can wait that long,' said the friend.

The wife could not persuade him to go away and so she had to show him into the friend's room. The ill friend was lying under a blanket, his face covered and only his toes showing at the end.

'I am here to wait,' the friend said. 'When you are better we shall be able to divide the money that those people gave us.'

The friend in bed said nothing.

*   *   *

As the day wore on, it became hotter and hotter. The friend under the blanket began to feel as if he were in an oven, and then, at last, he had to throw the blanket aside to let cool air in.

'I am glad that you are better,' his friend said to him. 'Now we shall be able to divide the money.'

Reluctantly, because he knew that there was nothing else he could do, the friend retrieved the box and gave his friend his share of the money. The friend thanked him and said how pleased he was that his friend had recovered from his illness.

'You are fortunate to get better in two hours rather than two years,' he said. 'Perhaps it is the good hot air that cured you so quickly.'

*   *   *

The friend who had pretended to be ill buried

his share of the money in a tin box. Unfortunately for him, the box had a hole in it and when he dug it up the following month the ants had eaten it all. His wife told him that this is what happened to people who obtained money through tricks.

'The ants like to play tricks too,' she said. 'It is your own fault for being such a wicked trickster.'

The other friend fell into a large hole on his way home from collecting the money. He was unable to get himself out of it and so he was very pleased when he saw some people walking by. These people were the people who had been under the tree.

'Please pull me out,' the friend called. 'I shall die if I am left down here.'

The people from under the tree looked down on the friend and agreed to pull him out. They would only do so, though, if he gave them money. The friend asked how much money they needed and they replied that they would want all his money. In this way the friend in the hole had to give the people from under the tree not only his share of the money he had got by trickery, but also his own money, which he had been carrying with him. In this way, too, the people from under the tree got back exactly that amount which they had given at the burial of the chief. If the chief had been alive to see all this happening he

151

would have said that this was the right outcome.

How A Strange Creature Took The Place Of A Girl And Then Fell Into A Hole

The daughter of the chief of some people near Kezi was one of the most beautiful girls in the whole of Matabeleland. The chief knew that there would be no difficulty in getting a good husband for her, but he did not want to leave anything to chance. Calling on a powerful witchdoctor, he asked him to provide charms that would be sure to attract a handsome man to the house.

The witchdoctor told the chief that this was not a difficult thing to do. The best way of attracting a handsome husband was to find a special tree, part of which would have been burned. From the burned part the girl should take a piece of charcoal and then rub this between her palms. If she did this, there would be no difficulty in finding the best possible husband.

The chief was pleased with this advice. He ordered his men to prepare food and water for a journey and then he set off with his daughter in the direction indicated by the witchdoctor.

It was harder than he had imagined to find the special tree but eventually they came to a valley where the conditions seemed right for the growth of such a tree. The chief climbed up to the top of a small hill at the entrance to this valley and looked down onto the place where he thought the tree might grow. When he saw it was there, he called out to his daughter and together they walked to the foot of the half-burned, half-green tree. Climbing up into the branches of the burned part, the chief broke off a piece of charcoal and brought it down to his daughter. She rubbed the charcoal between her palms and as she did so she described the sort of husband for whom she longed.

*   *   *

The girl's mother was waiting for them when they arrived home.

'A very handsome young man has arrived,' she told them eagerly. 'He said that he had lost his way and needed to be given directions to get to the Limpopo River.'

'It is my husband!' the girl shouted out gleefully. 'Please show him to me immediately!'

They took the girl to where the young man was sitting on a small rock and showed him to her. She was very pleased to see how handsome and strong he was and the father lost no time in telling the young man that he should marry his daughter. The young man said that he was happy to do this, but that he had no house of his own.

'That does not matter,' said the chief. 'I shall give you some poles and some thatch and you can go and build it.'

The young man asked whether it would be possible for him to build his house near the house of his own father, who lived by the Limpopo River. This was some distance away, but the chief agreed that this would be quite all right, as the father of the young man was a well-known chief in that part and he would be able to protect the girl from some of the dangers that were in the Limpopo River and nearby.

The chief spent a day discussing the house and the marriage with the young man and then sent him on his way.

'Begin the building of the house,' he said to him. 'In a month I shall send my daughter down to join you at your father's house. Then you can get married.'

*   *   *

It was difficult for the girl to pass the time without thinking constantly of the husband who awaited her. Toward the end of the month, her mother became ill, and she spent much of her time at her bedside, nursing her

155

and encouraging her to get better. The old woman, however, became weaker and weaker, although she was still able to tell her daughter how happy she was that she would soon be joining her new husband. At last the month had passed and the daughter was told that she could prepare herself for the journey. The chief fetched an ox for her to ride upon, and then he stood at the gate to bid her farewell. As she rode past him, he gave her a small flower.

'Watch this flower,' he said to her. 'If the flower wilts, then you will know that your mother has died.'

The girl began her journey, wondering if she would ever see her mother again. By midday, she was halfway there and paused to shelter for a while under the shade of a thorn tree. It was while she sat there that the flower, which she had been grasping in her hand, suddenly withered. At this, the girl knew that her mother had died and she began to weep.

It was important to that girl that her tears should not touch the ground. As the daughter of a chief, this would have been wrong, and so she quickly sought a place where she could weep in safety. Near the thorn tree was a deep ant-hole, and the girl sat next to this, allowing her tears to disappear into the dark depths of the earth. Unknown to her, a strange animal lived in that hole, and he soon felt the warm tears falling upon his skin.

At first the girl was frightened when the strange animal came out of the hole, but when he spoke to her and reassured her she was no longer afraid. He asked her where she was going and why she was going there, and when she explained to him he quickly suggested that it would be better if he accompanied her on her journey. The girl was pleased to have company, and so she agreed that the strange animal could come with her, at least as far as the hills near her future father-in-law's house.

While the girl rode comfortably on the ox, the strange animal loped along beside her.

'Your clothes are very beautiful,' he said to her. 'I wish that I had clothes like that.'

The girl felt sorry for the strange-looking animal and offered to allow him to try on her clothes for a short period. He was very pleased with this offer and was soon dressed in the girl's clothes, smiling to himself in his satisfaction. After they had covered a short distance, he looked up at the girl and asked her if she was comfortable on the ox.

'It is very comfortable,' the girl said. 'It is much easier than walking.'

The strange animal looked sad.

'I have never ridden an ox,' he said. 'I shall never know what it is like.'

Hearing this remark, the girl leapt off the ox and told the strange animal that he should take her place.

'This is very kind of you,' said the strange animal, smiling as he climbed onto the back of the ox. From where he sat, he could see the cattle pens of the father-in-law's village and he knew that they would soon be there.

*   *   *

The father-in-law was at the outer fence, ready to meet his new daughter-in-law. As the ox stopped in front of the village, the father-in-law stepped forward to help the strange animal get off the ox. He frowned as he did so, wondering to himself why his son had said that his new bride was so beautiful when in reality she was so ugly. Perhaps she will seem more beautiful tomorrow, he said to himself.

The real girl tried to tell her father-in-law that the strange animal was only a strange animal dressed in her clothes, but he refused to listen to her, thinking that she was only a servant girl. Telling her to keep quiet, he took the two of them to a hut he had prepared and there they were told to sleep.

The girl soon cried herself to sleep, but the strange animal nosed about the hut looking for things to eat. When he came across the calabashes of sour milk which the family kept in that hut, he drank them greedily, making a loud noise as he did so.

The next morning the family was surprised to find that their sour milk had all disappeared, but everybody thought that the calabashes must have leaked. New calabashes were obtained and these were filled with sour milk and put in the same place as the old ones. That night the strange animal again nosed about the dark corners of the hut and drank all the sour milk, turning the calabashes upside down to empty out the last drop.

The father was suspicious when he found that all the sour milk had once again disappeared and so he called everybody into the meeting area in front of his hut and told them of a plan he had.

'We have a sour milk thief among us,' he said gravely. 'There is only one way to find out who it is.'

In the middle of the village a deep hole was dug. Into the hole four calabashes of sour milk were placed and then everybody was ordered to stand in a line. One by one, the people of the village and the visitors too were forced to jump over the hole. Most landed safely on the other side and were told to stand to one side.

When it came to the turn of the strange animal to jump, he had almost reached the other side before he tumbled down into the hole. When the people looked down to see what was happening, they saw the strange animal drinking greedily. The temptation of

159

the sour milk had clearly been too much for him, and he had given himself away.

The father-in-law lost no time in ordering the hole to be filled in, burying the strange animal from sight. When this had been done, he turned to the girl and asked her to tell him what had happened. She told him how the strange animal had supplanted her and how nobody had been prepared to listen to her explanation at the beginning. The father-in-law realized that what she said was true and made it up to her by giving her many presents. When this happened, the girl almost entirely forgot about the strange animal and all the unhappiness which it had caused her.

Greater Than Lion

The hare did not like the lion. Every day the lion would walk about the bush, roaring. This frightened all the smaller animals, who feared that the lion would eat them. Even when the lion was not hungry he would roar, as if to say: 'There is no greater animal than I. All animals should bow down before me.'

It was true that there was no animal stronger than the lion, with the exception, perhaps, of the elephant. The elephant, though, was a shy creature. He disturbed nobody and would never walk round roaring. And if an elephant was ever attacked by a lion, there is no doubt that the elephant would retreat rather than stay and fight.

At last the hare decided that he must do something to stop the lion's constant bragging. He thought about it for over three days and just when he was about to admit that there was nothing that could be done, he had an idea. When the idea came to him he leapt up for the joy of it, just as hares are seen to leap in the early morning.

'Oh lion,' he said to himself. 'You will regret your boasts.'

When the lion saw the hare coming towards him, he rose to his feet and let out a mighty roar. The hare felt the ground shake under him and he wondered whether he shouldn't run straight home. But he continued to approach the lion with the roars ringing in his ears like thunder.

'How dare you walk up to me like that,' the lion shouted as the hare approached him. 'Don't you know who I am? Don't you know that I'm the mightiest of beasts?'

The hare drew himself up to his full height and addressed the lion.

'Oh lion,' he said. 'I know that you are a mighty beast. I know that all the animals in the bush are frightened of you.'

The lion seemed pleased to hear this and dropped his voice a little.

'Well,' he said. 'At least you show me proper respect. But why have you come to see me?'

The hare looked carefully at the lion, knowing that what he was about to say was dangerous for him.

'I have come to tell you,' he began, 'that there is a creature who is greater than you.'

When he heard these words, the lion roared again—a louder roar than the hare had ever heard. It seemed to him that the noise would knock him over and he cowered until the lion had stopped for breath.

'I don't mean to insult you,' he said apologetically. 'I just came to tell you.'

The lion stared down at the small creature in front of him.

'Show me this animal,' he said. 'Let me see him.'

The hare was relieved. 'I can show you,' he said. 'But you will only be able to see him in a house.'

'Then I shall go to this house,' roared the lion. 'Take me there right now.'

*   *   *

The hare led the lion along the path to the house that he had specially prepared for him.

'You must go into that house,' he said, pointing to the front door. 'Then you will see the creature that is greater than you.'

The lion bounded straight into the house and was quickly followed to the front door by the hare. Once the lion was safely inside, the hare bolted the front door and waited outside. Soon there came a thumping on the door as the lion realized that he was locked in.

'Where is this creature?' he shouted. 'Fetch him at once.'

'Keep calm,' called out the hare. 'You'll see him soon. Just wait for him.'

The lion went into the back room of the house and lay down on the cold stone floor. He waited all that day and all that night. The next morning the hare arrived at the front door and called out to the lion.

'Have you seen that creature yet?' he asked.

From within the house there came the sound of the lion's roar.

'No,' he said. 'I am the only creature here.'

'He will come,' promised the hare. 'Just you wait.'

The morning after that the hare returned at the same time and called out again to the lion.

'Is he there yet?' he asked.

This time the lion sounded angry. 'No,' he roared. 'And let me out. I've had enough of this.'

The hare ignored the lion's shouts and just laughed in reply.

'Just wait,' he said. 'Your visitor will come soon enough.'

*   *   *

Many days passed before the hare came back again. This time, when he called out, at first there came no reply from within the house.

'Lion,' he called out. 'Are you inside?'

After a few moments he heard a sound from the back room. It was not a great roar—it was more like the sound made by a tiny creature

164

that lives among the leaves and twigs. Cautiously the hare opened the door and went into the house.

He found the lion lying on the floor of the back room. His tongue was out of his mouth, parched with thirst, and his ribs showed on his sides. He was so weak from the days without food and water that he was unable to raise his head to look at the hare. Only his eyes moved as the hare came up to him and peered into his face.

'I see that your visitor has come,' the hare said. 'The creature greater than you came after all.'

The lion's eyes widened slightly.

'Who is he?' he asked in a tiny, weakened voice.

The hare laughed.

'Hunger,' he replied.

Head Tree

A man who had never done any wrong to anybody else had a great misfortune happen to him. His wife noticed that a tree was beginning to grow out of his head. This was not painful to the man, but it made him feel awkward when there were other people about. They would point at him and say that this was a very strange thing to happen. Some people walked some miles to see this man sitting outside his hut with a tree growing out of his head.

At last the man decided that it was time to do something about the tree. He asked his wife if she would chop it down, but she warned him that this could be dangerous.

'If this tree is growing out of your head,' she said, 'then you might bleed to death if I chop it down.'

The man agreed that this was a danger. So instead of chopping the tree down he went to see a certain woman who was well known in that part for being a woman who could use charms to solve difficult problems. This woman lived in a hut some distance away and so the man had to bear the stares of all the people as he walked to her place.

The charm woman looked at the man and said that she had never seen this sort of thing before, but that her mother had told her that things like this could happen and had given her instructions as to how to deal with it.

'You must have done something bad to have this happen to you,' she said.

'I have not done anything bad,' said the man hotly. 'I have always behaved well.'

'In that case,' said the charm woman, 'you must have been planning to do something bad. If this were not so, then why would a tree grow out of your head?'

The man had no answer for this, and so the charm woman took a special herb out of her bag and gave it to him.

'You must eat this every day for a week,' she said. 'At the end of the week the tree will go. You must also pay me two cows, for this is a very expensive herb and it is not easy to stop trees growing out of people's heads.'

The man promised that he would give the woman her cows once the tree had gone. Then he returned to his home and took the first part of the herb. At the end of the week, when he had taken the last part of the herb, the tree fell off his head. The man's wife chopped it up and they used the wood for their cooking fire. The man was very relieved, and he was now able to walk about without people pointing at him and clicking their tongues in amazement.

'You must give that woman her cows,' his wife said. 'She has cured you well.'

'I shall not,' said the man. 'She is just an old witch with a sharp tongue. There is no reason to give her anything.'

The charm woman heard that the tree had fallen off the man's head and she sent a young boy to tell him to send her two cows. The man listened to the message which the boy brought, but all he did was beat the boy with a stick and send him home.

The next day, when the man was sitting in front of his hut drinking his beer, his wife came to him and looked at the top of his head.

'Another tree seems to be growing,' she said. 'This time it looks very big.'

The man's heart filled with despair. He could not face the thought of having a tree on his head again, and so he went back to the charm woman's house.

'I have come for more medicine,' he said. 'And I have brought those two cows I promised you.'

The charm woman looked at him and shook her head.

'You are a wicked man who does not keep his promises,' she said. 'If you want me to cure you again and to stop that tree forever, you will have to pay me four cows.'

The man stamped his feet on the ground, but he knew that she was the only woman who could stop a tree from growing out of his head. Reluctantly he brought four cows and left them in front of her house. She gave him the herb and told him that he should always keep his promises, even if he thought that he had made a promise to a weak old woman. The man said nothing, but he knew that what she said was quite right.

The Grandmother Who Was Kind To A Smelly Girl

A beautiful girl had a very handsome makgabe, which is the apron worn by very young girls. This had been made for her by her grandmother, who was very kind to her. The grandmother had spent many hours weaving this makgabe for the girl.

The other girls in that place were jealous of that makgabe. Their own aprons were fine, but not so fine as the apron that that girl wore. They looked at her makgabe and thought that it would be better for them if they could get rid of it. But how do you take a person's clothes when that person is wearing them? That is a very difficult thing, even for clever girls.

One morning the girls invited that girl to go swimming with them in a river nearby. When they arrived at the river bank, the other girls said that they would all need to take off their makgabes, as the cloth would be damaged if it got wet. So all the girls did this, including the girl with the very beautiful makgabe.

When they were all naked, they jumped into the water and splashed around for some time.

Then they emerged and the leader of the jealous girls took the makgabe of that girl and threw it into the river, near a place where a very large snake lived on the river bank. Then all the other girls put on their makgabes and walked home, leaving that girl crying by the river, saddened by the loss of her beautiful apron.

The large snake heard her weeping and came out to see what was happening. When he saw this beautiful girl, he slithered out and swallowed the makgabe and the girl. Fortunately for her, the snake did not like the taste of the makgabe, and he spat both it and the girl out, leaving them lying on the bank covered with the slime which is to be found in a snake's stomach. This slime smells very bad.

The girl put on her fouled makgabe and ran home to her parents, singing:

Mother, open the door for me, I am smelling;
Mother, open the door for me, I am smelling,
　　　I am smelling very bad.

The mother heard this song and ran out of their house to sing back to the girl before she could come in:

Go away, you are smelling,
Go away, you are smelling,
Go away, you are smelling very bad.

The girl was very upset by this, and ran off to the house of her aunt and uncle. They heard her singing her song as she approached. They ran out, as had her mother, and sang the same song that her mother had sung, telling her to go away because she smelled so bad.

The poor girl then had only her grandmother's house to go to. She set off in that direction, her heart heavy within her. It seemed as if nobody wanted to look after her now that she smelled so bad. But she was wrong. When she reached her grandmother's house, the old woman did not send her away, but took her in and washed her, and her makgabe, making everything smell sweetly. Then the girl stayed there and some years later she received a proposal of marriage from the son of a very rich chief. The parents heard about this and asked her to come back to their house and live there. The girl, however, remembered how they had behaved when she had smelled so bad, and so she told them that she would never go back to their house, even if they were her parents.

'Parents must love their children,' she said, 'even if their children smell very bad.'

After her marriage, the girl invited the

grandmother to come and live with her in the house of this rich chief and his son. The grandmother was happy to do this, and she was very comfortable there, and very important.

The Baboons Who Went This Way And That

There was much unhappiness in a village of small huts. The people who lived there had been happy before, but then wild animals had come and had begun to frighten them. These animals ate all their crops and from time to time they even carried off children who wandered away from their parents. It was not a good place to live any longer, and the people began to think of where they might go to lead a new life.

One family found the answer. Rather than deal with the wild animals who seemed to be everywhere on the flat land, they decided to go in search of food up in the hills. It was not hard to find food there. There were bushes that grew in the cracks between rocks; there were trees that grew at the foot of the slopes; there were rock rabbits which could be trapped and birds which could be brought down with the stones which littered the floor of the caves.

Other families noticed how well the hill family was doing. They saw the sleekness of their children, and they noticed how calm the parents were.

'It is a good life that we lead up in the hills,' said the husband. 'You should come there too.'

Soon the other families abandoned their homes on the flat land and went up to the hills. Each family found a cave to live in, and in this way they were warm and secure. Soon everybody talked about how sorry they were that they had not come to the hills earlier, rather than letting the wild animals eat their crops and drag off their children.

As the children grew up in the hills, they began to get better at the things that had to be done to live in such a place. They became very quick at climbing rocks, and even the youngest could scamper up a face of rock almost as quickly as any rock rabbit. They also became good at climbing into trees to look for fruit, and they could swing in the branches almost as well as any monkey. People who passed by and saw the hill people living on their hill wondered whether they were perhaps wild animals, but when they saw their faces and the clothes that they were wearing they realized that they were only people who had made the hills their home.

Slowly, things began to change. The parents noticed that their children were talking less, and that rather than speaking to one another in the language of people they were beginning to use grunts. Then the adults themselves noticed that their noses were getting bigger and that they were growing hairier. Every time they looked at one another they saw that their faces had changed yet more and that their teeth were longer. Soon they spent as much time on four legs as on two, and it was at this point that they became a new creature. This creature, which had never before been seen in that place, was the creature which people now call the baboon.

For a time, the baboons lived happily. They stopped chasing the rock rabbits and started to eat grubs from the ground. They also forgot how to talk, and nobody now made any sound other than a bark or a grunt. They took off their clothes and let the rags lie on the ground until they were destroyed by ants. Their legs and arms were now completely covered with dark hair.

They still remembered, though, that they had been people, and this was something which made them worried. When they looked into each other's faces, they realized that their noses were now much bigger than they had been before, and this made them jeer. Every baboon laughed at other baboons, pointing at his enlarged nose and throwing his hands about in mirth. This made the baboon who was being laughed at angry. He would jump up and down in anger, all the while laughing at the large nose of the other.

Eventually the mockery became so great that the baboons could no longer bear to be together. Each family split off and lived by itself, laughing at the others because of their great noses, but not liking to be laughed at for their own noses. That is why baboons live in small groups today and do not live as a baboon nation, as do men and many other animals.

Two Friends Who Met For Dinner

A man once asked a friend to have a meal with him. The friend was happy to receive this invitation, as he was never asked by anybody else to go anywhere. He spent a great deal of time making sure that he was smartly dressed for the meal so that his friend would be proud of him.

The guest arrived at his friend's house and was asked inside. Together they sat at the table and smelled the delicious smell of the food that had been cooked.

'All the food is in this calabash,' said the host. 'To get it out, you have to put your hand in the neck and take out a piece. I shall show you.'

The host inserted his hand into the thin neck of the calabash and took out a morsel of food. It looked good, and the guest began to feel his mouth watering. Reaching across, he put his hand into the calabash and picked out a piece of food. Unfortunately, when he tried to take out his hand he found that it was too big to pass through the neck of the calabash with food in it. In order to get his hand out, he had to leave the food inside.

The host appeared not to notice the

difficulty in which his guest found himself. He had small hands, and so he was able to take food out and put it into his mouth. He did not offer to give any food to his guest, although he handed him the calabash again and told him to help himself.

After a few minutes, the host had eaten all the food. He looked at his guest and smiled.

'I am sorry that you did not get much food,' he said. 'But if you have big hands, then that is one of the things that happens to you.'

The guest said nothing. He was very sad that the only invitation that he had received for many years should have turned out to be such an unhappy occasion.

*   *   *

Some days later, the guest invited his host to dinner in his own hut. Before his friend arrived, however, he burned all the grass around his hut, so that the ground was black and charred with stubble.

The friend entered the hut and took off his hat.

'This is a good place,' he said. 'I am surprised that you do not have more friends, living in a comfortable place like this.'

The other man smiled.

'The food is ready,' he said. 'But first, if you don't mind, you must wash your feet. People do not like dirty feet in this place.'

The guest understood, and immediately walked off to the river to wash his feet. Then, when they were quite clean, he returned to the hut and found that the host had already started the meal. The host looked at the guest's feet and shook his head.

'I'm afraid that your feet are still very dirty,' he said. 'You will have to return to the river and wash them again. This is very good food here and I do not want it spoiled by dirty feet.'

The guest knew that this was right, but he could not understand why his feet were so dirty after he had washed them so carefully. This time, he ran to the river's edge and washed both feet thoroughly. Then, checking to see that they were quite clean, he ran back to the hut. On his way, of course, he passed through the middle of the charred stubble that surrounded his friend's hut. This soon covered his feet and made them dirty again.

'Oh dear,' said the friend. 'I must ask you to wash your feet one more time. Look at how dirty they are.'

The friend was now becoming angry, but he ran back to the river and washed the dirty feet again. Then he returned to the hut.

The friend looked at him.

'I'm sorry,' he said. 'I have just finished all the good food I prepared for the meal. Also,

I'm very sorry to tell you, your feet are still dirty.'

The Thathana Moratho Tree

A certain man liked trees. He had many trees in the ground behind his house, and he was very proud of these. There were trees for all purposes—a tree to attract birds that might sing well; a tree that had good branches for making fires; a tree that would keep away snakes because they were frightened of it. There were many trees, and the people in that place would come and look at them from time to time and wish that they had trees like his.

There was one tree that this man had planted which nobody else had in their yard. This was the thathana moratho tree, and he had given very strict instructions that nobody at all, not even his children, should ever touch this tree. Nobody knew why they were not allowed to touch this tree, but since the tree belonged to this man they accepted the rule. They could look at it, though, and many people did this, wondering what was so special about this particular tree.

This man had a child called Ntshetsanyana, who was looked after by a servant girl. One morning the child was very hungry and cried and cried for food. The servant looked for food with which to feed her charge, but found none. Eventually she went out into the yard, picked some of the fruit from the thathana moratho tree and gave it to the child.

The child said, 'What is this very good fruit?'

The servant girl replied, 'It is the fruit of the thathana moratho tree and you can eat it. I am telling you to eat it. I have picked it for you because you are so hungry and have been crying so much. Now you must eat it.'

The child took the fruit from the servant girl and ate it. It was very good, and the child smiled happily after the last morsel had been consumed. It was the best fruit that had ever been brought into the house, and the child hoped that there would be more chances to eat this fruit in the future.

When the man came back to his house he discovered what had happened and he was very angry. He shouted at the servant girl, who wept and cringed. The man told her that by feeding his child fruit from the thathana moratho tree, she had insulted him. Now he would have to take her to Chief Mmeke, who was a very stern chief. He knew the chief would kill both the girl and the child for doing this prohibited thing.

They set off together, with the servant girl carrying the child and the man driving them on, muttering to himself about the great insult that had been done him by this act of disobedience. On their way, they met a friend of this man, who asked them what was happening. The man explained about the insult, but the poor girl replied with a song:

He is lying: I did not insult him.
I only took thathana moratho;
I gave it to Ntshetsanyana
Who was crying.
Now I am to be taken to Mmeke,
Mmeke the ruthless one.

The man, however, did not wish to listen to her and he pushed her with a stick, making her continue her journey to the place of Chief Mmeke, where she would be killed.

Some time later, while still walking under the burning sun, they met the son of Chief Mmeke. He asked what was happening and the girl immediately sang him the same song. This time, the song was believed and the chief's son, a kind young man, fell in love with the girl. He said that he would go with them to the chief's place, although he did not say what he was planning to do once they got there.

'Do not kill this girl, Father,' said the young man. 'She is very beautiful and I wish to marry her.'

The chief listened to this, and then he listened to the man who had brought the girl to be killed. After the man had finished speaking, the chief said, 'Go home now, and leave this bad girl here. She will be killed tonight, when it is dark.'

The man was satisfied with this and he went away. They did not kill the girl, though: the chief's son married her and she became a very good wife for him. They had many fine sons, and she was very popular with Chief Mmeke himself, who was pleased that he had been kind to this girl.

Tremendously Clever Tricks Are Played, But To Limited Effect

There was a terrible drought once, with all the land crying out for water and the sky quite empty of clouds. The people stood and thought about rain, which they had almost forgotten, so long ago had the last rains fallen. And it was very bad for the animals too, who had to look in all sorts of places for water. They began to die, falling to the ground and staring up with lifeless eyes at the sky from which no water came.

Eventually the animals decided to hold a meeting. They all came together, walking slowly because of their thirst, and they talked to one another about what might be done.

'We must dig a well,' said Hyena. 'That is the way to get water when there is no rain.'

Of course it is easy for people to dig a well, as they have hands that can work the earth. But for animals it is a hard task, as they must scrape at the soil with their feet; it is slow, slow work for them. But all the animals did their part of the work—all except for Hare, who was lazy. When asked why he was not helping to find water, he replied that his family totem was water and therefore he had no need to drink. 'You must drink,' he said, 'but I do not need to. I shall watch you work.'

The animals were very fortunate in finding a good supply of water under the ground. They all drank their fill and then began to leave the well. When they returned, though, they found that the water was dirtied—somebody had been drinking from it in their absence.

'We must leave somebody on guard,' said Elephant. 'Then that animal will be able to stop the water from being dirtied while we are off hunting.'

It was agreed that Hyena would take on this task on the first day, and he was duly left there, while all the others went off in search of food. He sat in the shade of a tree and thought about things that hyenas like to think about, which are not things that you and I would understand.

After a short while he heard somebody coming. This person was singing, and it turned out to be Hare himself. 'I am very happy,' he sang. 'Some boys have dug a well for me/ Now I can drink and wash in the water to my heart's content/ I am a happy hare.'

Hyena was furious, and charged at Hare. Hare dodged his charge and then came towards him slowly, offering him a large piece of honeycomb. Hyena, who was greedy, took the honey and ate it all, while Hare sneaked off behind him and drank and washed in the water.

When Hyena saw that he had been tricked in this way, his heart burst within him, so great was his anger. Then he died.

When the animals came back, they were saddened to see that the water had been so dirtied. They found the body of their friend, Hyena, and many of the animals wept for him, as even an animal like Hyena is loved by some.

The next day Jackal offered to stay behind and guard the water. 'I am a very cunning creature,' he said. 'Nobody will be able to trick me.'

Hare came by again. This time he threw pieces of meat in front of Jackal, who ate them all up. The meat was delicious, and there was a great deal of it. As a result, Jackal became too fat to run after Hare as he went to the water and drank half of what was there and dirtied the rest.

On their return, the animal were furious with Jackal who had failed in his task all because of his greediness. They decided that the only thing to do was to kill him and to leave a girl in charge of the water.

'A girl will not be fooled so easily,' thought the animals. 'It is easy to fool animals, but a girl is different.'

Once the animals had gone away again, Hare sauntered along and told the girl that if she tried to stop him he would punch her with his hare fists. The girl said that this would not worry her, and so Hare punched her with his right fist. This fist stuck to the girl, and so he punched her with his other fist, and again the same thing happened. This left hare with his head as the only weapon at his disposal. But his head stuck to the girl too, and it was at this point that the animals all came back and saw the wicked hare stuck to the girl. They decided that he must be killed for taking their water.

'The only way to kill a hare,' said Hare, 'is by hare tradition. This means that you will have to swing me round and round and then smash me to the ground. That is the way it must be done.'

The animals agreed to this and Elephant, who was the strongest, was given the task of swinging Hare round and round with his trunk. But as he did so, Hare slipped out of his skin and sailed away in the air. When he landed safely, he turned and laughed at the animals, saying that they were perfectly welcome to kill his skin if they wished. So he ran off, laughing, although he had no skin now.

Hare did not return. The girl who caught him was praised by all the animals, and was allowed to share their water. This made her happy too.

CHIVERS LARGE PRINT –direct–

If you have enjoyed this Large Print book
and would like to build up your own
collection of Large Print books, please
contact

Chivers Large Print Direct

Chivers Large Print Direct offers you
a full service:

• Prompt mail order service

• Easy-to-read type

• The very best authors

• Special low prices

For further details either call
Customer Services on (01225) 336552
or write to us at Chivers Large Print Direct,
FREEPOST, Bath BA1 3ZZ

Telephone Orders:
FREEPHONE 08081 72 74 75

PK	09/05
LE	12/07